DISSOLVING THE EGO, REALIZING THE SELF

ALSO BY DAVID R. HAWKINS

Healing and Recovery

Reality, Spirituality, and Modern Man

Discovery of the Presence of God

Transcending the Levels of Consciousness

Truth vs. Falsehood

I: Reality and Subjectivity

The Eye of the I

Power vs. Force*

Along the Path to Enlightenment*

Orthomolecular Psychiatry (with Linus Pauling)

*Available from Hay House

Please visit:

Hay House USA: **www.hayhouse.com**®
Hay House Australia: **www.hayhouse.com.au**
Hay House UK: **www.hayhouse.co.uk**
Hay House India: **www.hayhouse.co.in**

DISSOLVING THE EGO, REALIZING THE SELF

CONTEMPLATIONS FROM THE TEACHINGS OF DAVID R. HAWKINS, M.D., Ph.D.

Edited by Scott Jeffrey

HAY HOUSE, INC.
Carlsbad, California • New York City
London • Sydney • New Delhi

Published in the United States by: Hay House, Inc.: www.hayhouse
.com • *Published in Australia by:* Hay House Australia Pty. Ltd.:
www.hayhouse.com.au • *Published in the United Kingdom by:* Hay
House UK, Ltd.: www.hayhouse.co.uk • *Published in India by:* Hay
House Publishers India: www.hayhouse.co.in

Editorial supervision: Jill Kramer • *Project editor:* Shannon Littrell
Design: Jenny Richards

The author of this book does not dispense medical advice or pre-
scribe the use of any technique as a form of treatment for physical,
emotional, or medical problems without the advice of a physician,
either directly or indirectly. The intent of the author is only to offer
information of a general nature to help you in your quest for emotional, physical, and spiritual well-being. In the event you use any of
the information in this book for yourself, the author and the publisher
assume no responsibility for your actions.

Library of Congress Cataloging-in-Publication Data

Hawkins, David R.
  Dissolving the ego, realizing the self : contemplations from the
teachings of David R. Hawkins, M.D., PH.D. / edited by Scott Jeffrey.
-- 1st ed.
      p. cm.
  ISBN 978-1-4019-3115-5 (tradepaper : alk. paper) 1. Self-realiza-
tion--Religious aspects. 2. Self--Religious aspects. 3. Spiritual life.
I. Jeffrey, Scott. II. Title.
  BL624.H356 2011
  128--dc22

                              2010051682

Tradepaper ISBN: 978-1-4019-3115-5
Digital ISBN: 978-1-4019-3116-2

1st edition, August 2011
5th edition, March 2013

Printed in the United States of America

Gloria in Excelsis Deo!

CONTENTS

Note: References to the Map of Consciousness and the concept of calibration are explained in detail in Dr. Hawkins's book *Power vs. Force* (Hay House, 2002).

PREFACE

All life reflects the evolution of consciousness, from that of the simple bacteria to the advanced levels of Enlightenment of the world's
Great Sages. Scott Jeffrey has taken on the formidable task of delineating core comprehensions
that occur along the Great Pathway. These selections are inspirational, innately transformative
steps that accelerate the journey to Enlightenment. To completely understand any one of them
illuminates all the others. It is the great journey
that uplifts the reader from the seemingly mun-
dane to the Realization of the Glory of God.

— **David R. Hawkins, M.D., Ph.D.**

INTRODUCTION

The contemporary spiritual student is bombarded by information and activities that consume time and attention. This collection of writings on the nature of ego, mind, and consciousness itself is designed to be a pocket companion for serious seekers and students of Dr. David R. Hawkins's teachings, easily portable and taking up little room on your nightstand. Whether you're working at your desk, waiting in line at the bank, sipping coffee in a café, hiking in the woods, or just lying in bed, *Dissolving the Ego, Realizing the Self* provides convenient contemplations of Truth.

Quotes and passages to inspire contemplation and reflection for the student on the go have been hand-selected from all of Dr. Hawkins's core writings—including *Power vs. Force; The Eye of the I; I: Reality and Subjectivity; Truth vs. Falsehood; Transcending the Levels of Consciousness; Discovery of* the Presence of God; and *Reality, Spirituality, and Modern Man*—as well as numerous other published and unpublished works.

The chosen selections have been taken directly from the above sources, with only minor alterations where appropriate, categorized topically for the reader's convenience, with a great deal of overlap between sections. The beauty of this format is that you may begin reading wherever you feel most inspired, or simply flip to a page at random. (If you find that any of the terms used are unfamiliar, please consult the Glossary at the back of the book.)

The approach to spiritual progress as explained by Dr. Hawkins isn't one of "getting somewhere," as there is no "where" to get. Instead, you're guided to transcend your ego and shed all illusions so that Truth stands revealed. As he explains in many of his talks, "The sun is always shining; you need only remove the clouds."

Dr. Hawkins's teachings expose the ego/mind as nothing more than a complex house of mirrors. As a skilled teacher and mystic, he guides us out of perceptual distortions and fallacies into the Light of Consciousness itself. His teachings represent a beacon of truth that any willing spiritual aspirant can follow to higher levels of consciousness.

You'll find that Dr. Hawkins illuminates the illusion of duality (the sense of separation of a "this" observing a "that") and the true nature of Subjectivity, Reality, and Truth with a precision unsurpassed in spiritual literature. He offers the devoted student the gift of clarity and spiritual direction, distilling difficult and confusing topics for the Western mind.

Dr. Hawkins's teachings are not oriented toward the spiritually timid; that is, those more interested in energizing belief systems, confirming opinions, and blindly adhering to ecclesiastic doctrine. For the individual who is honestly moving toward greater meaning and understanding, and ultimately Self-realization, the passages herein were selected.

In transcending the illusion of the (small) self, one realizes the (higher) *Self*—the Ultimate Reality out of which consciousness arises, beyond words or concepts. The first section of this book explores the true nature of the small self—the ego and mind. Subsequent sections are devoted to transcending that self and experiencing the nondualistic Presence of Divinity and the realization of Enlightenment.

Many of the themes and concepts presented in this book are repetitive, as they are in Dr. Hawkins's core writings. This is done intentionally, as Dr. Hawkins explains that nonlinear principles are learned through repetition rather than linear, sequential understanding. It is in reading, rereading, and contemplating the meaning behind the words that one's understanding ripens. Eventually, the teaching becomes a part of the student (a subjective, experiential reality). Words, then, become unnecessary.

May your spiritual journey lead you to Higher Truth. . . .

— Blessings,

Scott Jeffrey

Part I

THE "SELF" (EGO/MIND)

The process of transcending to the highest levels of enlightenment is one of letting go of the identification of a personal self. The belief in an "I" or "me"—a central processing unit that has its own body, mind, and emotions—is a hindrance to realizing one's true nature. Dr. Hawkins explains that the self (with a small "s")—the composite of ego and mind—presumes there is a centralized "inner primary causal agent, for example, the 'doer' of deeds, the 'thinker' of thoughts, and the 'decider' of decisions." We start by exploring the nature of the ego and the mind—the sense of a personal self— so we are better prepared to transcend this misidentification.

1

NATURE OF THE "EGO"

Hawkins describes the ego as "the imaginary doer behind thought and action." This "set of entrenched habits of thought," enforced by societal consensus and unconscious repetition, creates the illusionary sense of a personal self. The primary goal of spiritual work is to transcend the central processing unit believed to be essential for survival. Understanding the ego's nature reveals its underlying mechanisms so that we may withdraw the value we innocently projected onto it, thereby enabling spiritual progress.

The progress of consciousness is facilitated by an awareness of the evolutionary nature of the ego and its structure.

Realization is a progressive process. Spiritual progress is hastened by understanding the true nature of the ego. It is not an enemy to be attacked or defeated, nor is it an evil to be vanquished. It is dissolved by compassionate understanding.

In spiritual parlance, *ego* implies a negative quality, an obstacle to realization because of its linear dualistic construction. In psychology, however, the term denotes coping and survival skills needed to deal effectively with the world.

The world of the ego is like a house of mirrors through which the ego wanders, lost and confused, as it chases the images in one mirror after another. Human life is characterized by endless trials and errors while attempting to escape the maze. At times, for many people—and possibly for most—the world of mirrors becomes a house of horrors that gets worse and worse. The only way out of the circuitous wanderings is through the pursuit of spiritual truth.

Because the ego is constructed of positionalities, it has no option to be anything else except what it is. It therefore becomes an inescapable source of endless suffering and loss. Above all else, it fears the future and the specter of death itself, which is intrinsic to the ego's structure.

The ego is not an enemy to be subdued, but merely a compilation of unexamined habits of perception.

The ego can be thought of as a set of entrenched habits of thought, which are the results of entrainment by invisible energy fields that dominate human consciousness. They become reinforced by repetition and by the consensus of society. Further reinforcement comes from language itself. To think in language is a form of self-programming. The use of the pronoun *I* as the subject—and therefore the implied cause of all actions—is the most serious error, and automatically creates a duality of subject and object.

~~~~~

There is no such thing in reality as an ego; it is merely illusory. It is made up of a compilation of arbitrary points of view supplied by mental processing and powered by feelings and emotions. These desires represent the attachments that the Buddha spoke of as the bondage of suffering. With absolute humility, the ego dissolves. It is a collection of arbitrary mental processes that gain force only because of vanity and habit. If one lets go of the vanity of thought, it dissolves. All thought is vanity. All opinions are vanities. The pleasure of vanity is therefore the basis of the ego—unplug it and it collapses.

~~~~~

The ego is neither bad nor an enemy, but merely an illusion to release so that something far better can replace it.

~~~~~

The ego is the imaginary doer behind thought and action. Its presence is firmly believed to be necessary and essential for survival. The reason is that the ego's primary quality is perception, and as such, it is limited by the paradigm of supposed causality.

The ego fears dissolution and therefore resists giving up the illusion of a separate existence in an imaginary "here" and an imaginary "now." It fears it will dissolve into being nothing, and consequently the conscious awareness will also cease. With examination, it will become clear that one's reality is not a "who" at all, but instead is an intensely loving Allness, which is realized and known to be much closer and more comforting and fulfilling than the prior sense of "I."

The ego could be called the central processing and planning center—the integrative, executive, strategic, and tactical focus that orchestrates, copes, sorts, stores, and retrieves.

As we get closer to the discovery of the source of the ego's tenacity, we make the amazing critical discovery that *we are enamored with our self.*

The ego secretly "loves" and clings to the position of victimhood and extracts a distorted pleasure and grim justification from pain and suffering.

One mechanism the ego uses to protect itself is to disown the painful data and project it onto the world and others.

The ego is extremely tenacious and therefore often seems to require extreme conditions before it lets go of a positionality. It often takes the collective experience of millions of people over many centuries to learn even what appears to be a simple and obvious truth—namely, that peace is better than war or love is better than hate.

Although the critical level of integrity (level 200 on the Map of Consciousness) is the very threshold of spiritual progress, one can see that due to the structure of the ego, it can be difficult to achieve. The strength of the ego is such that it can be overcome only by spiritual power.

The ego has habitual modes of determining perception. They have to be identified first before they can be disassembled. One has to give up guilt about having an ego.

More important is not the nature of the ego, but the problem of identification with it as the "me," the "I," or "myself." The ego was inherited as an "it," and is actually an impersonal "it." The problem arises because one personalizes and identifies with it. That "it" of the ego structure is not unique or individual, and it is relatively similar (with karmic variations) in everyone. What really varies from individual to individual is the degree to which one is enslaved by its programs. The degree of dominance is therefore determined by the extent to which one identifies with it. Inherently, it has no power, and the power to decline the ego's programs increases exponentially as one progresses spiritually. That is the real meaning of the Map of Consciousness. What the majority of people think to be truth is, in reality, opinions.

From a greater context, we can view that the ego is not "evil," but is primarily a self-interested animal. Unless the "animal self" is understood and accepted, its influence cannot be diminished.

Curiously, the ego's hold is weakened by acceptance, familiarity, and compassionate understanding; in contrast, it is reinforced by self-criticism, condemnation, fear, and shame.

Temptation stems from within; it is merely the desire to experience the ego's payoff and satisfactions of an impulse, even if it is only a curiosity or a wanting.

The human ego likes to pretend that evil exists "out there" and seduces its hapless, innocent self into inadvertently falling into the trap of seduction. The real tempter is the ego's desire for gain—whether that be sensation, excitement, advantage, prestige, or the pleasure of controlling others.

The psychological source of seeming evil is primarily the naïve childishness of the primitive animal instincts of the infantile ego, which tends to go into a rage if its impulses are blocked by external authority. The same oppositional rage or narcissistic rebellion characterizes the criminal, the adolescent delinquent, the warmonger, and the puritanical moralist; they are all the same.

It is well to keep in mind at all times that the ego/mind does not experience the world, but only its own perception of it.

The ego is not the real "you"; it was inherited as part of being born a human. It basically originates from the animal world, and the evolution of consciousness happened through the primitive stages of mankind's evolution, so it could be said that to seek enlightenment is to recapitulate the history of human evolution.

～～～

The ego is a set of programs in which reason operates through a complex, multilayered series of algorithms wherein thought follows certain decision trees that are variously weighted by past experience, indoctrination, and social forces; it is therefore not a self-created condition. The instinctual drive is attached to the programs, thereby causing physiological processes to come into play.

～～～

The ego gets a grim pleasure and satisfaction from suffering and all the levels lacking integrity: pride, anger, desire, guilt, shame, and grief. The secret pleasure of suffering is addictive. Many people devote their entire lives to it and encourage others to follow suit. To stop this mechanism, the pleasure of the payoff has to be identified and willingly surrendered to God. Out of shame, the ego blocks out conscious awareness of its machinations, especially the secretiveness of the game of "victim."

※※※

Q: The programs of the ego do not continue unless they are secretly pleasurable?

A: That is the secret about secrets. The payoff is a gain of a pleasurably satisfying reward. The ego has learned to be very clever in order to survive. It is capable of resorting to any lengths or ruse of self-deception and camouflage. The world we witness is merely the drama of the collective egos acting out on the perceptual stage of form and time.

※※※

The satisfactions of the ego are more pleasurable and addictive than the preservation of human life, much less dignity.

※※※

By commitment to inner honesty, it will become apparent that the underpinning of the ego's responses is the pleasure that is derived from them. There is an inner satisfaction that is the payoff of self-pity, anger, rage, hate, pride, guilt, fear, and so on. This inner pleasure, as morbid as it may sound, energizes and propagates all these emotions. To undo their influence, it is merely necessary to be willing to forgo and surrender these questionable, inner secret pleasures to God and look only to God for joy, pleasure, and happiness.

To undo the ego, one must be willing to abandon this payoff game, with its grandstanding of emotions and repetitive rehashing of data and stories to justify its positions. One will note that the ego milks every wrong and that it has no greater pleasure than to indulge in "righteous indignation." It just "loves" that juicy positionality that has such a great payoff.

The ego's addiction and survival are based on the secret pleasure of negativity, which cannot be abandoned until it is first recognized, identified, and owned without shame or guilt. One has to see that this is just how the ego—which everyone inherits—operates, and recognize that it is not really personal at all.

———

To the ego, abandoning the self-reward dynamic is looked upon as a loss. The ego does not trust God and thereby thinks it has only itself to turn to for sustenance, survival, and pleasure. The ego has faith in its own mechanisms and not in God. It should not be faulted for this error because it has no experiential basis for comparison. Its only way out is with faith that there is a better way. It hears a spiritual truth and begins to search for it when the mind becomes disillusioned with its own fallacies and failure to achieve happiness. It finally realizes that the grim satisfaction it squeezes out of pain is a poor substitute for joy.

———

To the ego, gains lie without; to the spirit, they are internal, for the ever-present joy of existence is independent of content or form. To the spirit, a sunny day or a rainy day are the same. Awareness enjoys qualities rather than grasping at form. Thus, it can enjoy "being with," without having to own or control. Awareness is not driven by goals but instead values the capacity for equal pleasure in all circumstances.

The ego's rigidity and resistance to correction are based on narcissistic egotism, pride, and vanity. The collective egos of whole nations bring about their downfall and destruction.

The ego is not only unable to correctly assess situations that are fatal, but it even willingly sacrifices life for its own ends. The ego is therefore potentially deadly and would rather "see you dead" than admit it is wrong.

The ego conceals, whereas awareness reveals. The answer to many defective ego positions could be subsumed in the commonly overlooked sanity of "common sense."

At the higher levels, the ego is seen to be an illusion, without any innate reality.

~~~

At its roots, the ego is the extreme of self-ishness and is completely lacking in all ethical principles.

~~~

The ego is a victim of itself. With rigorous introspection, it will be discovered that the ego is really just "running a racket" for its own fun and games and survival. The real "you" is actually the loser.

~~~

The ego clings to emotionality, which is intimately connected with its positionalities; it pretends to think that it has no other choices. To "surrender to God" means to stop looking to the ego for solace and thrills and to discover the endless, serene joy of peace. To look within is to find the underlying, ever-present source of the illumination of the mind itself.

~~~

The ego defends its own limitations with prideful denial, thus becoming its own victim.

～～～

From a developmental analysis, which utilizes consciousness-research techniques, it appears that the human ego itself is primarily the product and continuation of the presence of the survival core of the animal evolution.

～～～

In contrast to the innate arrogance of the ego, true intelligence is a quality of consciousness/ awareness and is not subject to attack because its essence is nonlinear. It is, however, utilized by the ego in its expression as mind, which then be- comes and subserves the ego's drive for survival. Thus, the ego really uses the mind as camouflage and becomes hidden in its clever constructions. This recognition clarifies why the ego's masquer- ade as religion and the undermining of spiritual truths have been central to its domination of large cultures for extended periods of time and the deaths of millions.

～～～

The persistence of the primitive ego in man is referred to as the narcissistic core of "egotism," which, at calibration levels below 200 (the critical level of integrity), indicates the persistence of the primitiveness of self-interest, disregard for the rights of others, and seeing others as enemies and competitors rather than as allies. There is nothing deadlier than the religionized ego.

While the ego/self routinely takes credit for survival, its true source is the presence of Divinity as Self. It is only because of the Self that the ego is capable of being self-sustaining. It is just a recipient of life energy and not its origin, as it believes.

The ego is the main hero/heroine in the inner movie of one's life.

The clever ego expresses its inner grandiosity by seeking to replace Divinity by declaring itself to be God (or Nero, Caesar, and so on), or claiming special Divine authority by its declaration that it is Divinely ordained and therefore authorized.

Ego positions have the characteristics of disowning responsibility and placing blame "out there." In the end, the ego's payoff is the energy by which the ego persists, because it lacks the pleasure of the input of spiritual energy. The ego's payoff is its substitute for Divinity; thus, it maintains its sovereignty and is convincing in its secret, silent belief that *it* is the source of one's life itself—that is, that *it* is God.

On its own, the ego would never seek salvation . . . the mechanism for salvation is via the will, which invites the intervention of Divinity.

To the ego, a "want" is interpreted as a "need" and a "have to have." Thus, its seeking can become frantic, and all caution can be thrown to the wind. Desires are thereby escalated to being desperate and demanding any sacrifice, including even the deaths of *millions* of other people. It *must* have what it wants at any cost and will find many excuses to justify itself. It gets rid of reason with clever rhetoric bolstered by blame and demonizes others, for the ego has to *win* at all costs—because throughout millions of years of evolution, it *did* die if it did not get its wants and needs fulfilled. The ego has a long, long memory and millions of years of reinforcement.

The ego structure is dualistic and splits the unity of Reality into contrasting pairs and seeming opposites that are therefore the product and content of perception, which consists of projections.

The ego's position propagates itself because its secretly sought payoff is the emotion itself.

The inflated ego is devoid of reality testing as well as amelioration by reason, logic, or rationality.

Addiction to the ego's proclivities is like intoxication where pleasure is derived from the emotional payoff of negativity. Thus, negative positionalities tend to be self-perpetuating habits akin to addiction, based on presumptions and the inner seductive lure of the gratification of basic animal instincts. By repetition, they eventually gain dominance and control, which is the innate purpose of the narcissistic ego in the first place.

The levels below calibration level 200 (the critical level of integrity) tend to be self-propagating because of the seductive emotional pleasure of the ego's animal-instinct payoff.

The ego is oriented toward specifics and the linear content of the field of vision. Its effect on vision itself is exclusive and limited in order to focus primarily on the near side of objects (so as to facilitate manipulation). Spirit is oriented toward context and the whole, and is thus inclusive and focused on the far side of objects. Its field is diffuse rather than local.

In ordinary life, the ego/mind goes from "unfinished" to "finished," and then from "incomplete" to "complete." In contrast, the spiritual pathway is a direction and style that goes from complete to complete as evolutionary states of emergence. Ego positions are interactive and usually represent a composite. For example, to disassemble anger may require the willingness to surrender the pride that underlies that anger, which in turn depends on surrendering a desire. This means surrendering the fear that energized the desire, which again is related to the undoing of imaginary loss, and so forth.

Motivations are thus intertwined and mutually interactive, and operationally surrendering them leads to the next levels, which are comprised of dualities. Thus, the deeper layers tend to surface one's belief about God, programmed spiritual expectations, and belief systems. Spiritual work is therefore a matter of exploration that transcends mental concepts, such as those of cause and effect.

The ego's survival relies on the defeat of truth because it is dependent on allegiance to falsity. For one thing, spiritual truth challenges the ego's presumption that it is sovereign.

The ego is addicted to being "right" (for example, politics). A prevailing goal of the ego is to be "right." Therefore, it is the core of the payoff of righteousness. You can be right without being righteous, and you can be righteous without being right.

The ego is focused on one point, the experiencer, which is programmed to seek pleasure and survival through gain. It views happiness as something one acquires, possesses, and incorporates. Therefore, the experiencer is programmed to "get." The experiencer's function is to get pleasure and possess it. It is not concerned with the soul unless it fortuitously becomes spiritually oriented. Then its goals shift, and it discovers that the source of pleasure is completely within. When it is discovered that the source of ongoing pleasure is the Self (and not the small self), the result is independence from the world. Gratification of the ego's desires is within the linear domain. True happiness arises from the nonlinear. With relinquishment of dependence on the experiencer for pleasure and happiness, one discovers that the source of happiness is one's own existence, and the realization of the Self is happiness itself.

Notice that the experiencer aspect of the ego is constantly poised to derive benefit from the witnessed phenomena, even if it is only to confirm its own reality as being the "you" of the ever-presumptuous personal "I."

The ego is reluctant to accept that the unfolding of sequential phenomena is autonomous and impersonal. It is poised to jump in to impose a feeling, which in turn is always the expression of an ego viewpoint or positionality, such as an opinion, or at least an order to declare itself to be primordially essential to one's identity and sense of reality. To cease identifying the experiencer as the reality of oneself is a major transition from dualistic content to nondualistic context, and therefore, from self to Self.

The ego is not the actual reality or source of life or existence, and is therefore vulnerable to dissolution. It is primordial but not essentially sovereign. It is dominant only until its illusory quality is recognized.

The body itself is actually not experienced; instead, only the *sensations* of the body are experienced. Therefore, awareness of the body is merely a composite sensation by which the somatic area of the brain records input, and by neuronal function, replicates the body image.

The attachment to the body is to sensation and the superimposition of the concept of "mine"; what is "mine" and is controlled by "me" must therefore be "who I am." Identification with the body is consequent to the ego's positionalities. To detach from identification of the self as the body, it is necessary only to see the body as an "it" rather than a "me."

The sense of "who" we are is primarily an identification with the body, the personality, and its mental processing, with accompanying emotional investment. One can do an internal mental imaging process to see how much of the body or its sensations could actually be lost and yet have the self retain a sense of "I." It becomes clear that the experiential "I" *has* a body but *is not* a body.

The narcissistic core of the ego is aligned with being "right," whether being "right" means being in agreement with wisdom or rejecting it as invalid. With humility, the serious searcher discovers that the mind alone, despite its education, is unable to resolve the dilemma of how to ascertain and validate truth—which would require confirmation by subjective experience as well as objective, provable criteria.

There is a secret payoff and satisfaction in being the victim, martyr, or loser.

As Freud discovered, out of guilt the animal nature of man becomes repressed and then projected onto others, or onto a deity that purportedly has the same character defects as man. Historically, man paradoxically fears his own projections and confuses Divinity with the repressed dark side of his own nature. The ego is dissolved not by denunciation or self-hatred, which are expressions of the ego, but by benign and nonmoralistic acceptance and compassion that arises out of understanding its intrinsic nature and origin.

It is well to remember that the human psyche is like the hardware of a computer, which innocently accepts any software with which it has been programmed. This was stated by Socrates as "all wrongdoing is involuntary, for man always chooses what he believes to be for his good." Man is merely mistaken in what is really the source of goodness and happiness and thus mistakenly chooses externals (illusions) instead of Truth. Instead of vilifying the ego—and indulging in guilt, shame, and self-hatred—it is far more productive to accept it for what it is, appreciate its historic value, and adopt it as one would a naïve pet.

We can accept that the ego is, "of course," desirous of gain, advantage, greed, and the like. By simply expecting it to be as it is, its nature can be accepted and then transcended. The ego just does what it has been trained to do over the millennia, and it still thinks that its survival depends on adherence to, and the practice of, its programs. Because of evolution, these programs have now become the antithesis of the intentions of the ethical person of today or of the serious spiritual seeker.

In approaching the ego, it is well to remember that it feeds off of, and is seduced by, the energy of the negativity of pain, suffering, hate, and guilt—to which it then gets attached (addicted). It secretly nurtures the "juice" it gets from being the martyr or the victim; and it loves hatred, being "right," and revenge. The consciousness level of the ego is based on the utilization of the qualities of force, whether they are emotional, intellectual, or physical. The undoing of the ego, consequently, is not by the utilization of moralistic or emotional counterforce but by use of the power of Truth itself.

* * *

The primary underpinning of the persistence of negativity is the ego's secret payoff from negativity ("juice"). This secret payoff is the ego's only source of energy, so it sees forgiveness, as well as compassion, as the "enemy."

⁓

The self identifies not only with the mind, but also with its content—which becomes "my" memory, "my" senses, "my" thoughts, "my" emotions, "my" property, "my" success, "my" failure, "my" expectations, "my" feelings, and so on. Identification presumes ownership and authorship; thus, the ego sees and believes itself to be a personal, separate causal agent and the inferred source of its own existence.

⁓

Intrinsic to the very basic construction of the human ego is an innate innocence in that it believes in the reality or truth of its own programs and is unaware that it lacks an intrinsic capacity for self-correction. The reason for the ego's inherent lack of capacity for verification is that its data is limited to only internal processing systems. The internal mechanisms of the ego lack any external, independent source of reference for verification.

With compassion, one realizes that the structure of the ego is such that it cannot know what
lies beyond.

There is no timetable or prescribed route to
God. Although each person's path is unique, the
terrain to be covered is relatively common to
all. The work is to surmount and transcend the
common human failings that are inherent in the
structure of the human ego. One would like to
think that these failings are personal; however,
the ego itself is not personal. It was inherited
along with becoming a human being. Details dif-
fer based on past karma.

The vanity of the ego (at the level of pride)
is endless and vainglorious in its grandiose delusion that it can disprove the existence of God.
Cognition is only linguistic supposition confined
to linear symbols, the limited content of mental
processing. That it has any actual objective reality at all is a purely subjective presumption.

By spiritual endeavor, one discovers that it is *oneself* who has been a captive and a "victim" ensnared by the clever deceptions of the ego.

All the great teachers have declared that man's primary defect is "ignorance." Research reveals rather quickly that the underlying basis of this ignorance is due to the limitation of the innate structure of the ego itself as a consequence of the still-ongoing evolution of consciousness.

In the human, there evolved not only the capacity to process and interpret linear data, but there was also available the nonlinear energy of consciousness/awareness that was called "spiritual" because the energy source was nonphysical and not definable by linear concepts. This, too, was evolutionary in its human development and was called the "human spirit." It was characterized by the emergence of a nonphysical ("etheric") energy body, the survival and evolution of which were independent of the physical body itself. Thus, spirit is related to essence, and reason to linear form and definition.

As can be seen from its evolutionary development, faith was a biological necessity for survival that was built into a basic structure of the ego as the sense of self. The capacity to be aware of and experience the self was a quality of sentient awareness innate to the animal kingdom. Thus, humankind lived by faith. Naïvely, the ego placed its primary faith in the narcissistic core of the ego itself (for example, perception and opinion), which therefore assumed autonomy and sovereignty as the arbiter of reality. The ego is, by virtue of its structure and origin, blind to its own limitations.

The absolute subjectivity of revealed Truth precludes all considerations or uncertainties which stem only from the ego. When the ego collapses, all argument ceases and is replaced by silence. Doubt *is* the ego.

That the mind is unable to prove a proposition does not mean that the proposition is false.

This is the pitfall of the atheist because the mind is unable to know what is true. It is simultaneously equally unable to disprove it, for it would then be in the paradox of having to prove its opposite. The narcissistic core of the ego unconsciously and naïvely presumes that it is omnipotent and therefore lacks the humility that is requisite to arriving at higher Truth.

Paradoxically, benefit is derived by the self-interest of the ego when it begins to realize that there is a great advantage to unselfishness. When it learns of the benefit of letting go of egocentric goals, the ego itself then becomes the springboard to spiritual inquiry and the means to its own transcendence, realizing that humility is strength and not weakness, and that it is wisdom and not ignorance. The willingness to "forgive and forget" calibrates at 450 (reason/logic). The willingness to "forgive and surrender to God" calibrates at 540 (unconditional love).

2

NATURE OF "MIND"

Often used interchangeably with "ego," "mind" is the processing unit with which the ego is identified. Ultimately, like the ego, the mind itself is only a concept. As Dr. Hawkins explains, "Experientially, one can only state that thoughts, feelings, images, and memories come into one's awareness in an endless progression." And it is this endless progression that we've come to call "mind." As one comes to understand the true nature of the mind, one becomes less at the effect of its inner workings and better positioned to transcend to one's identification with it.

Like the body, the mind is not one's real self, and like the body, it is basically impersonal. It has thoughts, but these thoughts are not a product of the self. Even if a person does not want a mind, he or she has one anyway. There is no choice in the matter; the mind is imposed and thrust upon one unasked. The fact that having a mind is an involuntary imposition helps with the realization that it is not a personal choice or decision.

All seeming separation is an artifact of thought. It is essential to see that the mind is at all times experiencing a point of view.

The design of the human mind is comparable to that of a computer in which the brain is the hardware capable of playing any software programs fed into it. The hardware is, by design, incapable of protecting itself from false information; therefore, the mind will believe any software program with which society has programmed it, for it is innocently without any safeguard or protection.

The human mind, by virtue of its innate structure, is naïve, blind to its limitations, and innocently gullible. Everyone is the victim of the ignorance and limitation of the human ego.

The human mind is incapable of discerning truth from falsehood. Were this not so, there would have been no wars in history, no social problems, and no ignorance or poverty. Everyone would be enlightened, and the consciousness level of mankind would not have remained at 190 (the level of pride, below the critical level of integrity at 200) on the Map of Consciousness, century after century.

Because of dualistic perception, the mind could no longer discern the abstract symbol from reality. The road to error was open and inviting, and opinion held sway, as the mind had no innate mechanism to discern truth from falsehood. As a result of dualistic mental processing, the mind had developed the capacity for repression and denial so that it could remove obstacles to achieving its goals. The mind discovered that it could deny ownership of an unwanted side of a pair of opposites and project it onto the world. Thus were born not only politics but also the well-known psychological mechanisms of splitting, repression, denial, and projection. This capacity turned out to be a fatal mechanism in that even when faced with dire results, the ego relentlessly pursued the same mistakes. Millions of people die in every generation throughout history and continue to do so in today's world.

Except in small, personal affairs, the mind was not constructed to readily learn from its mistakes.

One is not "forced" to feel resentment by a negative memory, nor does one have to buy into a fearful thought about the future. These are only options. The mind is like a television set running its various channels for selection, and one does not have to follow any particular temptation of thought. One can fall into the temptation of feeling sorry for oneself, or feeling angry or worried. The secret attraction of all these options is that they offer an inner payoff or a secret satisfaction that is the source of the attraction of the mind's thoughts.

One thing is obvious: the mind is totally un-reliable. It cannot really be depended upon at all. It is not able to be consistent, and its performance is sporadic as well as erratic. It will forget to take the keys to the office, forget telephone numbers and addresses, and be the source of frustration or annoyance. The mind is contaminated by emo-tions, feelings, prejudices, blind spots, denials, projections, paranoias, phobias, fears, regrets, guilts, worries, and anxieties; along with the fear-some specters of poverty, old age, sickness, death, failure, rejection, loss, and disaster.

In addition to all the foregoing, the mind has also been innocently and erroneously pro-grammed by endless propaganda, political slo-gans, religious and social dogmas, and continual distortions of facts—not to mention falsifications, errors, misjudgments, and misinformation. Above all else, the primary defect of the mind is not only its content, which is often irrelevant or in error, but the fact that it has no means of telling truth from falsehood. It is merely a game board.

Humility is of greater value than all factual accumulation. Unless one has completely and totally experienced the presence of God in its stunning, absolute Allness, it is safe to assume that one really knows nothing and that all accumulated so-called knowledge is really only tentative. Anything within that claims "I know" proves that it is false by that very statement, or else it would not make such a claim.

Thinking proceeds from lack; its purpose is gain. In wholeness, nothing is lacking. All is complete, total, and whole. There is nothing to think about, nor any motive to think. No questions arise, and no answers are sought or needed. Totality is complete, totally fulfilling, with no incompleteness to process.

Beliefs are the determinant of what one experiences. There are no external "causes." One discovers the secret payoffs that are obtained from unconscious secret projections. One's underlying programs can be discovered by simply writing down one's litany of grievances and woes and then merely turning them around into their opposites.

Thoughts are occurring on their own, not because they are caused by anything or anyone.

Operationally, the mind is dualistic and thus sets up separate mental processing based on arbitrary, hypothetical positionalities that have no intrinsic reality. Thus, by design, the mind has the basic defect, as pointed out by Descartes, that it cannot differentiate *res cogitans* from *res extensa* (that is, mental activity about the seeming appearance of the world versus the world as it actually is). The mind thus confuses its own projections and mistakenly assumes that they have an external, independent existence—whereas, in reality, no such condition exists.

The mind translates phenomena in 1/10,000th of a second; thus, the mind is like the playback monitor of a tape recorder. When that interface of mind between phenomena and experiencing dissolves, the difference is quite dramatic.

The mind acts as a processor of data simultaneously from both within and without. It categorizes, sorts, prioritizes, contextualizes, and interprets simultaneously as it concordantly draws on memory banks, emotional centers, and conditioned responses and their correlations. All the above are orchestrated contextually with emotional/animal instincts that are sorted, rejected, accepted, or modified.

In addition, this profound complexity is simultaneously subject to options, choices, and the will. Options and choices are related to meaning and value overall—and they are under the influence and dominance of an all-inclusive, overall field of consciousness having concordant and variable levels of power related to the level of consciousness that is also influenced by karmic propensities. Simultaneously, the mind assesses degrees of relative truth, credibility of information, and suitability and probabilities of action within similarly multilayered behavioral social limits, including moral, ethical, social, and religious principles.

⁓

The mind is like an infinitely complex processing unit of both internal and external data.

⁓

The mind naïvely assumes that it is the real "me" who is searching for truth because it assumes that its ego/self is primary and is the sole author of intention as well as action, and therefore the arbiter of reality.

⁓

A person identifies with his body because his mind is *experiencing* his body.

⁓

The end point of intellectual investigation arrives at the obvious conclusion that the mind and the intellect are each inherently defective and therefore incapable of arriving at absolute truth.

Q: *What makes thinking so tenacious?*

A: All mental content represents attach-ments, and underlying are the attachments to the self and the clinging to what is believed to be the source of survival as well as happiness. It is also one's identification. In reality, the source of happiness is the Self, and not the self (the ego).

Thinking is a processing device with great pragmatic value; it presumes that it knows the data, but it actually has no innate capacity to know. Belief manufactures an imaginary inner "knower" that becomes the "me." Likewise, it manufactures an imaginary doer of deeds, an actor of acts, and an imaginary thinker of thoughts.

Each thought actually arises out of nothing-ness, or the black field of silent mind, and is not, as presumed, caused by a preceding thought.

Consciousness research confirms that approximately 99 percent of the "mind" is silent and only 1 percent is processing images. The observer self is actually hypnotized by that 1 percent of activity and identifies with it as "me"—it is oblivious to the silent 99 percent of the field because it is invisible and formless.

Once thoughts or feelings are labeled as "mine," they become magically imbued with presumptive omniscience and an assumed sovereign validity.

Thoughts, ideas, and concepts are of pragmatic and useful value to worldliness; but with the relinquishment of worldliness, they are excess baggage and of no value.

Through self-examination and inward focus, one can discover that all states of consciousness are the result of the execution of an option. They are not unchangeable certainties determined by uncontrollable factors at all. This can be discovered by examining how the mind works.

The primary defect now is, as it always has been, that the design of the human mind renders it intrinsically incapable of being able to tell truth from falsehood. This single, most crucial of all inherited defects lies at the root of all human distress and calamity.

The ego/mind presumes and is convinced that its perceptions and interpretations of life experiences are the "real" thing and therefore "true." It also believes by projection that other people see, think, and feel the same way—if they do not, they are mistaken and therefore wrong. Thus, perception reinforces its hold by reification and presumptions.

The dualistic proclivity of the mind prevents the realization of the Oneness of Reality or the occurrence of Self-realization because the dualistic belief system as represented in language presumes a "this" causing a "that." It therefore simultaneously and automatically also views the self as being a separate (and moralistically judged) "doer of deeds." This dualistic system of mental processing reinforces the ego's position-alities that, in turn, produce the perceptual "illusion of the opposites" that stands at the gateway to enlightenment.

Although the human mind likes to believe that it is "of course" dedicated to truth, in reality, what it really seeks is confirmation of what it already believes. The ego is innately prideful and does not welcome the revelation that much of its beliefs are merely perceptual illusions.

The human mind presumes that the commonality of a belief system is evidence of truth, and, of course, history is full of obvious examples of the contrary (for examples, see *Extraordinary Popular Delusions and the Madness of Crowds* by Charles Mackay).

Just as the physical "I" registers images and objects like a camera, the mind is the "I" of the self, which perpetuates the illusion of a unique, separate personal identity that becomes hypothecated to be the originator of thought, intention, desire, and so on. With relinquishment of this narcissistic illusion, it becomes apparent that all aspects of supposedly personal life are actually occurrences that are autonomous and spontaneous.

All negative emotions persist because of their secret payoff. When this "ego juice" is declined, thoughts tend to diminish and then disappear. The mind then tends to "go blank," which then brings up the fear of boredom. With observation, it becomes clear that the mind is busy anticipating the future (fear); clinging to the past (regret, hatred, guilt); or savoring the past to extract pleasure via reruns. Thus, the mind becomes the focus of amusement as "doing" something.

Because consciousness is formless and devoid of content, it is able to recognize form. Thoughts are only discernible if they move in a field of non-thought. The background of the mind is therefore the silence of the field of consciousness itself. In turn, consciousness, which is a field of potential energy, is detectable because it is illuminated by the light of awareness that is the Self.

The mind has only information and imagination *about* anything; it cannot actually "know" because to know is to be that which is known. All else is only speculation and supposition. When the mind is transcended, there is nothing left to ask about. That which is complete lacks nothing, and that completion is self-evident in its Allness.

Although the personal self likes to think that the thoughts going through the mind are "my thoughts," they are actually only "the thoughts" that prevail at a given level of consciousness.

Thoughts think themselves; they don't need you at all, just like the body goes about its business on its own.

The mind's reality is a fiction. With that realization, it loses its reign as the arbiter of reality. Through the eye of the ego, life is a kaleidoscope of consciousness-changing attractions and repulsions, fears and transient pleasures.

If you watch what your mind is really doing, you'll see that it is always trying to get "one up" on the next instant. By the next instant (about 1/10,000th of a second), what a person is experiencing (they are never experiencing reality) is the ego's interpretation of reality. Like an audio system, there is a monitor. So just as you record a program, the monitor feeds it into your ears. You heard what was just recorded a split second ago, but you are not hearing the program source; you are hearing what was just recorded.

Most people experience the monitor tape of the ego's interpretation of events. They're not experiencing events as they are in reality; they're experiencing the ego's interpretation.

Mentalization is of egocentric origin, and its primary function is commentary. Unless requested, thought is vanity: an endless procession of opinion, rationalization, reprocessing, evaluating, and subtle judgment by which the thoughts are given value or importance via presumed significance because they are "mine." The ego is enamored of its life story and its central character.

That the human mind, without help, is unable to tell truth from falsehood due to its own innate structure and design is so staggering a discovery that it is roughly comparable to the discovery by Copernicus that caused cultural shock in the 16th century. Because this single fact alone is confrontational to the average mind, it will probably not be welcomed or warmly greeted by those who profit from sophistry and its illusions.

Part II

TRANSCENDING THE SELF

As Dr. Hawkins explains, when the self (ego/mind) is transcended, Truth stands revealed. There are various pathways to Truth and Self-realization, including the pathways of mind, devotion, meditation, and contemplation. Each pathway emphasizes a different approach or style to arrive at the same end. This section addresses different avenues Dr. Hawkins has emphasized for Self-realization.

3

PATHWAY OF MIND

The "pathway of mind," also called the "pathway of no mind," is the pursuit of Truth via knowledge—through a thorough examination of the illusionary nature of ego and mind and their various programs. Enlightenment, then, occurs through a letting go of these false programs, whereby one experiences a realization of what is. In these contemplations, Dr. Hawkins provides the spiritual aspirant with clear direction to navigate out of the ego's "house of mirrors."

The very process of studying the mind already begins to diminish the ego's grip. The sense of self begins to shift locus, and the feeling of one's inner "I" begins to progress through the layers of consciousness.

In actuality, the ego-self doesn't have to die at all: life doesn't come to an end; existence doesn't cease; and no horrible, tragic fate is waiting to end life at all. Like the ego itself, the whole story is imaginary. One doesn't have to destroy the ego or even work on it. *The only simple task to be accomplished is to let go of the identification with the ego as one's real self!*

With this relinquishment of identification, the self actually goes right on walking and talking, eating and laughing—the only difference is that, like the body, it becomes "that" instead of "me" or "this."

All that is necessary, then, is to let go of ownership, authorship, and the delusion that one invented or created this self and see that it was merely a mistake. That this is a very natural and inevitable mistake is obvious. Everyone makes it, and only a few discover the error and are willing or able to correct it.

The ego is not overcome by condemnation, hatred, and guilt. Rather, one de-energizes it by viewing it objectively for what it truly is—that is, a vestigial remnant of man's evolutionary origins.

One is not really ruled by the mind at all. What the mind reveals is an endless stream of options, all disguised as memories, fantasies, fears, concepts, and so on. To get free of domination by the mind, it is only necessary to realize that its parade of subjects is merely an arbitrary cafeteria of selections wending their way across the screen of the mind.

Radical humility can be arrived at only by confining thoughts and opinions to their verifiable validity. This means the willingness to let go of all presumptions of thought. With persistence, the vanities disappear as truths and are now seen as the basis for errors. In one final, glorious crash, one realizes that the mind doesn't really "know" anything. If anything, it knows only "about," and it cannot really know—because to really know means to *be* that which is known (for example, to know about China doesn't make one Chinese).

~~~

To limit the mind to what is provably known is to reduce it in size and influence so it becomes one's servant and not one's master. It becomes obvious that the mind actually deals in presumptions, appearances, perceived events, nonprovable conclusions, and mental activities that it misidentifies as reality. No such reality as that constructed by the mind actually exists.

~~~

When carefully examined, one finds that all opinions are worthless. They are all vanities and have no importance or intrinsic merit. Everyone's mind is loaded with endless opinions, and when seen for what they are, opinions are really only mental activity. What is of more importance, however, is that opinions stem from and reinforce positionalities, and it is these positionalities that bring on endless suffering. To let go of positionalities is to silence opinions, and to silence opinions is to let go of positionalities.

Basic to the ego's continuance and capacity to dominate is its claim to authorship of all subjective experience. The "I thought" is extremely quick in interjecting itself as the supposed cause of all aspects of one's life. This is difficult to detect except by intense focus of attention during meditation on the origination of the thought stream.

The time lapse between an internally sensed occurrence and the ego's claim to authorship is about 1/10,000th of a second. Once this gap is discovered, the ego loses its dominance. It becomes obvious that one is the witness of phenomena and not the cause or doer of them. The self, then, becomes identified as that which is being witnessed rather than as the witness or experiencer. . . . In summation, it can be said that the ego is a compilation of positionalities held together by vanity and fear. It is undone by radical humility, which undermines its propagation.

To undo the dominance of mental content, it is necessary to remove the illusion that thoughts are personal; that they are valuable; or that they belong to, or originate from, one's own self. Like the body, the mind and its contents are really a product of the world.

⁓

The thought *I know* precludes the ultimate awareness of the real "I am." The word *know* is dualistic and assumes a dichotomy between a separate subject—the "knower"—and something external to be known.

⁓

Reality becomes self-evident when the obstructions of perception and mental activity are removed, including all belief systems.

⁓

It is not really necessary to subdue the ego, but merely to stop identifying with it.

⁓

Cease to identify with the body/emotions/mind as "me." Be truthful and admit that they are yours but not you. This may seem artificial, strange, foreign, and unnatural in the beginning;

yet the basic reality is that it is a truth of higher order, which makes it a very powerful and formidable tool. The mind will try to deny this reality as well as truth (that's what it is "supposed to do") because Truth is intuited as its nemesis.

Whereas ordinary information is "acquired" by effort, in spiritual endeavor the emphasis is on relinquishing, letting go, and surrendering. The "work" involves identifying positionalities and then transcending the ego's resistances and relinquishing its illusory control or sovereignty. Thus, the core of spiritual work is aligned with the undoing and unloading of the mind rather than its enrichment.

Complexity is a perception of the ego/mind. One sharp knife can cut through hundreds of different objects; there is only the necessity of one simple action. Analogously, there is only *one simple key concept* necessary to disengage from all the ego's encumbrances: it has only one addiction, which is subjective pleasure/gain. That is the secret payoff of *all* desires, projected values, and attractions. This is exaggerated by projected value, worth, glamour, or specialness. There is only *one* gain, and this same gain is merely superimposed on everything that is desired and therefore attracts attachment. The pleasure is associated with derived happiness; thus, the ego has only one goal. That discernment enables escape from all attractions. This solitary motive is merely projected onto multiple diverse objects, persons, qualities, events, or circumstances.

～～～

The clever ego can extract the juice/payoff of secret gratification and pleasure from anything it arbitrarily selects. Actually, it is always just the same goal over and over again. The "what" that is desired is actually irrelevant. The locus is imagined to be "out there" but is actually "in here," for the pleasure gained is subjective and internal. The relinquishment of this single, solitary goal unveils the Reality of the Self—which is the innate prime source of all happiness—and its Realization terminates all wants and desires. The locus of happiness is always solely from within. Pleasure is transitory; joy and happiness are from within.

The key to transcending the inherent limitations of the ego/mind is humility, without which the mind is hopelessly trapped in its illusory house of mirrors.

Once the evolutionary structure and function of the ego are understood, its disassembly is facilitated by the inner decision to pursue that which is real and eternal rather than that which is temporal, transitory, and ephemeral.

The human mind is like a ship at sea that is unable to correct its direction without a compass or an external source of reference, such as the stars. It is important to realize that a system is only correctible when it has access to an external point of reference (like a global positioning system) that serves as the Absolute by which all other data are compared.

To transcend the mind is to see that the many and the one are the same. Without the contrasting mental dualistic terms of *many* or *one,* neither would be said to exist. Instead, there could only be this realization: "All Is."

All opinions are vanities with no intrinsic value, and are actually the result of naïveté.

Whereas ordinary mental functioning could be typified as a constant effort to "get" something, spiritual realization is totally effortless, passive, and spontaneous. It is received rather than obtained. By analogy, when sound stops, the silence reveals itself. One cannot get it by effort or endeavor. With mental activity, there is a capacity to control; with revelation, there is no control at all. No control is possible where there is nothing to control and there is no means to apply control, even if it were possible. That which is formless cannot be manipulated.

From thinking that we *are* our minds, we begin to see that we *have* minds—and that it is the mind that has thoughts, beliefs, feelings, and opinions. Eventually we may arrive at the insight that all our thoughts are merely borrowed from the great database of consciousness and were never really our own. Prevailing thought systems are received, absorbed, and identified with; in due time, they are replaced by new ideas that have become fashionable with us. As we place less value on such passing notions, they lose their capacity to dominate us. We experience progressive freedom of, as well as from, the mind. This in turn ripens into a new source of pleasure; fittingly, the pleasure of existence itself matures as one ascends the Map of Consciousness.

Identification solely with the content of consciousness accounts for the experience of self as limited. In contrast, to identify with consciousness itself is to know that one's actual Self is unlimited. When such circumscribed self-identifications have been surmounted so that the sense of self is identified as consciousness itself, we become "Enlightened."

The mind, in its identity with the ego, cannot, by definition, comprehend reality; if it could, it would instantly dissolve itself upon the recognition of its own illusory nature. It is only beyond the paradox of mind transcending ego that that which *Is* stands forth self-evident and dazzling in its infinite Absoluteness. And then all these words are useless.

At all times, remain aware that the real you is not the ego. Refuse to identify with it.

By introspection, one can see that there is that which changes and that which is changeless. That which changes thereby identifies itself as illusion.

The mind can only "know about," rather than truly comprehend, essence—which is a nonverbal realization in which consciousness and essence are united as Oneness.

It is a relief to let the mind become silent and just "be" with surroundings.

The well-disciplined mind should only speak when requested to perform a task. Untrained, the mind becomes an unruly "onstage" performer and a nuisance. The self needs to learn respect for the Self and the silence of the Presence. By observing the mind, it becomes apparent that the self represents the disruptive, unruly child who constantly seeks attention.

It is usually fruitless to try to block thought, or to force the mind to be still without removing its motivation and payoff. Its motivational roots can be identified and surrendered. It is then surprisingly possible to make a decision: *Just do not think about anything.* This is made possible by aligning with the infinite silence out of which thinkingness arises. It is located not between, but just before, the emergence of thoughts.

The undoing of domination by the mind can be accomplished by one single step—humility—which is reinforced by simply recognizing that the mind is not sovereign, omniscient, or even capable of telling truth from falsehood.

Q: How can one silence the mind?

A: One cannot. It stops of its own accord when the energy of interest is removed. It is of greater service to merely disown it and stop identifying with it as "my mind." Thoughts are the automatic consequence of a specific calibrated level of consciousness plus personalization, by which they gain value. With relinquishment of the activation of memory, one lives in the emergent instant rather than hanging on to the past or anticipating the future.

The mind stops when it is no longer narcissistically energized. Thinkingness is intrinsically a vanity. Survival is spontaneous and autonomous, an automatic karmic consequence. Even when the mind becomes totally silent, the body goes about its business like a karmic windup toy.

<center>~~~~~</center>

Q: What replaces the mind when it disappears?

A: Divine wisdom unfolds. Consciousness/ awareness remains, but it is an autonomous quality or condition. Loss of mind does not result in "nothingness"; on the contrary, it is replaced by Allness. The leaf is not the tree.

It is safe to abandon any identification with what one thinks or believes one is, for none of it is real, and "nothingness" is purely an imagination.

<center>~~~~~</center>

All thinking, from a spiritual viewpoint, is merely vanity, illusion, and pomposity. The less one thinks, the more delightful life becomes. Thinkingness eventually becomes replaced by knowingness. That one "is" does not really need any thought at all. It is helpful, therefore, to make a decision to stop mental conversation and useless babbling.

To refuse memory, which is the vast store-house of illusions, leads to a clear approach to self-inquiry. It leads to the discovery that there is no actual "who"; there is only awareness. You're not a "who" but a "what."

To a highly aware person, most people seem to walk about as if they are in some kind of a dream state, unconscious and unaware of them-selves. Self-observation leads to awakening, which then motivates the desire to learn, grow, mature, and evolve. Self-inquiry leads to discov-ery and the unfolding of the layers that obscure the Self. With self-inquiry, one examines the basis for faith and beliefs—and by instituting spiritual techniques and criteria, one proceeds to discover the inner validation of spiritual truths for oneself. Thus, the field of inquiry is the func-tion of consciousness/awareness and the manner in which it contextualizes the inner experience of self, others, and Divinity.

The inner process is primarily one of de-energizing illusions rather than one of acquiring new information.

The "experiencer" is the perceptual edge of consciousness/awareness that is independent of the nature of the data being processed. It is this quality that one identifies with as "me" or "I." With observation, it will be recognized that this function is autonomous and impersonal, although the self claims it is identity. The experiencer is not a "who" but an "it." It is an autonomous functionality. It is comparable to a multifunctional processing-probe faculty. The ego/self thrives on that "experiencer" quality and is actually addicted to it.

By attention and volition, the seductive attraction of the experiencer can be refused. Succumbing to its entertainment is only a habit. It is not a "you," but only an activity with which the self becomes identified. The mind thinks that it will "go blank" and become void without the constant linear input of information and focus on "what's going on." Yet at night, sleep is a welcome relief from the experiencer's endless chatter. Thus, the mind thinks there are only three possibilities: (1) experiencing; (2) sleep (oblivion); or, perhaps, (3) sleep with dreaming. But relatively unknown to the ordinary mind is a fourth state, which is one of awareness itself, and independent of content or experiencing—or even participating, analyzing, or recording. The underlying quality is effortless, peaceful, and compatible with a contemplative lifestyle. It leads to the state classically termed as *samadhi*.

Once thoughts, like objects, are depersonalized, they become devalued and lose their attraction. Thoughts and feelings arise from desire, and the mind desires what it values.

To clear the mind, merely note that nothing at all is of special or unique "value" or "worth" except by invested, superimposed, and projected belief. Therefore, withdraw value, worth, importance, and interest.

The major transitions occur when conceptual thought is abandoned along with interest in "experiencing" or identification with the experiencer "edge" of the ego/self and its processing functions.

With practice, one can stay focused on the quality of consciousness as a process without actually getting involved in the "what" that is being processed or experienced.

Through observation, it can be seen that beneath the images and words themselves, there is a driving energy—a desire to think, to stay mentally active, to keep busy with any input the mind can find to fill in the gaps. One can detect a drive to "thinkingness," which is *impersonal*. With observation, one can detect that there is no "I" thinking the thoughts at all. In fact, the "I" rarely intervenes.

Spiritual reality is a greater source of pleasure and satisfaction than the world can supply. It is endless and always available in the present instead of the future. It is actually more exciting because one learns to live on the crest of the current moment, instead of on the back of the wave (the past) or on the front of the wave (the future).

There is greater freedom from living on the knife-edge of the moment than being a prisoner of the past or having expectations of the future.

If the goal of life is to do the very best one can do at each unfolding moment of existence, then through spiritual work, one has already escaped the primary cause of suffering. In the stop-frame of the radical present, there is no life story to react to or edit. With this "one-pointedness" of mind, it soon becomes obvious that everything merely "is as it is," without comment or adjectives.

When the mind stops talking, one is aware that one *is* life. One is immersed in it rather than being on the surface, talking about it. Paradoxically, this enables full participation. With diminution of egocentricity, the joy of freedom and the sheer flow of life sweep one into total surrender. One then stops reacting to life so that it can be enjoyed with serenity.

Spiritual progress is possible because the mind, through understanding, is able to recontextualize the contents of the ego and discern its very mechanism. Once this occurs, one is no longer blindly "at the mercy" of the ego.

As the payoffs of the ego are refused and surrendered, its grip on the psyche lessens, and spiritual experience progresses as the residues of doubt are progressively relinquished. As a consequence, belief is replaced by experiential knowledge, and the depth and intensity of devotion increase and may eventually supersede and eclipse all other worldly activities and interests.

Eventually, it is recognized that form is constituted by the formless and that they are one and the same—but until that realization occurs, form itself is a distraction and a delay that is best avoided.

Q: *How can one facilitate progress?*

A: That is a natural curiosity. Choice results in proclivities that become habitual mind-sets of attention. Within each moment are all the necessary elements for realization. Look for essence rather than just appearance. Everything is perfect if seen as it really is. Everything is exactly the way it is "supposed to be," whether it is shiny and new or rusty and dusty.

Avoid adjectives, for they are all projected, mentalized qualifications. Later, one can even drop verbs and adverbs for nothing is actually "doing" anything; it just innately *is*. Transition is a phenomenon that stems from within the observer who sees sequence as a verb. If seen in less than 1/10,000th of a second, everything appears to be stationary.

Error occurs when we cling to the belief that I *am* "that." Truth is unveiled when we see that one *has* "that" or *does* "that," instead of *is* "that."

There is great freedom in the realization that I "have" a body and a mind, rather than that I "am" my mind or body. Once the fear of death is transcended, life becomes a transformed experience because that particular fear underlies all others. Few people know what it is to live without fear. But beyond fear lies joy, as the meaning and purpose of existence become transparent. Once this realization occurs, life becomes effortless, and the sources of suffering dissolve; suffering is only the price we pay for our attachments.

A major deterrent to spiritual evolution and transcending identification of the self with one's mind is the processing of data, symbols, and words via random mentalization, which is presumed to be "thinking."

One has the illusion that one couldn't get through life unless one thinks. No such thing happens. It is not necessary for any individual to be there. It is not necessary to think that there is an "I" that is responsible for one's actions. Everything is doing itself. It is the vanity of the ego that says, "I did this; I thought that; I decided that." There is no such "I" at all. All these things are deciding themselves and doing themselves, all by themselves (autonomous). There is no necessity for an "I." There is no "doer"; all is "doing itself" spontaneously. There is no separate person doing anything; action occurs of itself. Objectification stops. Experience shifts from successive states to process itself, from linear to nonlinear; and objective and subjective are all one.

The ego/mind is afraid that if it doesn't think, it will (1) get bored, and (2) cease to exist. The problem of boredom is relatively easy to transcend simply by seeing that boredom is just the frustration of not being amused by "interesting" thoughts. To transcend the thinkingness, interest should really be refocused on searching for the substrate out of which thinkingness arises.

By understanding and accepting the nature of the ego, it is transcended and finally collapses and disappears when all of its positionalities and their resultant dualities have been surrendered.

The ego does not become enlightened, but instead disappears and collapses. It is then replaced by a Transcendental Reality as described by the Buddha; that is, the Buddha Nature. Just as the sun shines forth when the clouds disappear, the Reality of the Self shines forth of its own as Revelation, Realization, and Enlightenment.

4

SUBJECTIVITY

There is the objective world—the world perceived "out there"—existing in form, governed by time and space. Then there is the subjective experience—an internal state of being. How do you know that you are? That you exist? Dr. Hawkins points the student inward to the impersonal quality of consciousness and the field of awareness itself, which generally goes unnoticed because the ego/mind is focused on the content of phenomena being processed through perception.

The way out is simple: Direct one's focus inward to the absolute subjectivity of all experiencing. Examine the nature of the sense of subjectivity that accompanies every expression of life. Without labeling, note that at all times—in every instant, in every moment, in every circumstance—there is always present the ultimately irreducible, underlying substrate of subjectivity. It never changes. The essence of experiencing, in all its forms (thinking, feeling, seeing, knowing, and so on), is the presence of this subjective quality. Then look further to find out what this subjective experiencing is that is ever present. Without it, there would not be the possibility of knowing that one exists.

Ask, "How am I aware or even know that I exist?" That question is the best that can be acted upon, for it leads directly and nonverbally to the ever-present Reality. Identify with that quality, capacity, or condition of ever-present subjectivity, which is experienced as an underlying awareness. It is consciousness itself. Identify with that consciousness instead of with the "what" it is conscious about. That is the direct route to the Self. It is actually the only practice that leads directly through the doorway. There is nothing to know, to learn, or to remember. It is merely necessary to focus, fixate, meditate, contemplate, and look at—and to realize that the source and substrate of existence is the radical subjectivity of the Presence of God as the Light of Consciousness.

To accept the inner core of one's existence as a self-existent reality requires letting go of any definitions of oneself as a "who," and instead see oneself as a "what."

Simply put, realization or enlightenment is the condition where the sense of self moves from the limited linear material to the nonlinear infinite and formless. The "me" moves from the visible to the invisible. This occurs as a shift of awareness and identification from perception of form as objective and real to the realization of the purely subjective as the Ultimate Reality.

The realization eventually occurs that the "I" is not the content or the data, but an impersonal field several steps removed from the content of the programs. One then realizes that one is the audience, rather than the participant or subject.

※

To "know about" means that although the information itself is familiar, its reality and truth remain to be confirmed experientially. In the final stage of achieving certainty, to really know means to "be," and thus both subject and knower are unified. To know "about" is mental; to know experientially is accepted as confirmatory.

※

The field of conscious awareness is not time-tracked. It is silent, autonomous, effortless, peaceful, all-encompassing, and unprogrammed; it is free, unbound, spontaneous, tranquil, and not subject to birth or death. Discovery of this field is simple, easy, and relaxed. The realization is a consequence of "allowing" rather than "trying." It is surrendered to rather than acquired. As the desire for, and the ego's obsession with, control are relinquished, the field presents itself for recognition.

※

Q: *What is beyond mind?*

A: Subjective awareness devoid of content, such as thoughts, feelings, or images—silent, still, unmoving, All-Present, All-Inclusive.

Curiosity can be shifted from the form and content of thoughts in order to become aware of the silent nascent field of consciousness/awareness itself. Silence is of the Self; thoughts are of the self.

The ego/mind is attracted to novelty and therefore searches frantically for interesting form and sensation. This can be refused and replaced by interest in the silent, formless substrate that is always present and merely has to be noticed. It is comparable to the silent background without which sound could not be discerned.

Peace can be the consequence of surrender to the inevitabilities of life. The religious/spiritual skeptic can look within and observe that the inner fundamental and irreducible quality of life is the capacity of awareness, consciousness, and the substrate of subjectivity. Without consciousness, the individual would not "know"—or even "know" if he or she "knows"—so consciousness is *a priori* awareness of existence, irrespective of the content of that existence. Thus, consciousness itself can be accepted as an obvious reality, without the elaboration of being Divine (as recommended by the Buddha). To "be" is one thing; to *know* that one "is" obviously requires a more transcendent quality.

What gives the sense of "I" its subjective quality of reality is the radiance of the true Self, which is the source of the Reality that emanates as the Presence. To clarify the pursuit, it is helpful to search for the innate quality that accords the subjective experiential sense of identity itself. It may be more fruitful to search for the source of the quality of subjectivity, which is not a "who" but an innate quality of sentient life (a "what").

Is reality subjective or objective? At some point, the introspective mind ponders the truth of its qualities, that is: *How do I know? How do I know that I know? How do I know that which I presume to be truth is actually true?* In addition: *Whence arose life, and what is its source?* This subjective state is nonlinear, primordial, and *a priori*. Out of this impersonal field arises the very personal sense of "I-ness" as a primary quality of content. This basic subjective sense of "I" is capable of reflexive *self-knowing,* whereas, in contrast, the mind merely *thinks.*

The undoing of the identification of the ego/self is the primary focus of spiritual evolution and is the enigma that has baffled even the most erudite minds of history. The crux of the problem is misidentification with qualities of the ego/mind's processing function, which is already identified with the linearity of the localization of phenomena. This is a natural consequence associated with the physical reality of the experience of life as a body. The primary problem is misidentification of the actual source of subjectivity and the presumption that it is local rather than nonlocal.

In the process of spiritual discovery, one looks to discover what it is that is aware of—and has the authority to sense the existence of—"I-ness" or the quality of "I-ness," rather than a specific or circumscribed "me" as the "I."

All mental approaches to a definition of truth are eventually confronted by the necessity of making a paradigm jump from the abstract to the experiential, and from the supposedly objective to the radically subjective. Thus, the statement "Only the objective is real" is a purely subjective premise. Therefore, the mechanistic reductionist actually lives in an intrapsychic, subjective reality, the same as everyone else.

The resolution of the dilemma of a description and knowingness of absolute truth requires the leap into the field of research of consciousness itself—which makes it clear that the only actual, verifiable reality of knowingness is by the virtue of "being" (that is, all intellectualizations are "about" something). This requires that the observer be extraneous in order to be the witness of the thing to be examined. For example, a human observer can "know about" a cat, but only a cat really knows what it is to be a cat by virtue of the quality of *being* a cat.

5

WITNESSING AND OBSERVING

A form or style of contemplation that leads one to Self-realization is witnessing and observing. Whereas the ego is focused on the experiencing of sensations and the processing of experience, witnessing and observing shift the focus to an impersonal field of awareness, helping one transcend the attractions and aversions of the self through nonattached observation.

After one has observed the general field of mind, it is apparent that the specific content of the thought stream itself is not likely to be rewarding. One has to stand back and move further into the next level of consciousness and ask what is it that is watching, observing, being aware of, and registering the flow of thoughts. In the same way that the eye is unaffected by what is observed or the ear by what is heard, the ongoing process of witnessing is unaffected by that which is witnessed.

Just as there is no entity that is doing any thinking, there is no witness behind witnessing. Witnessing is an impersonal, inborn aspect and characteristic of consciousness itself. One can retreat from involvement with the contents of thought and choose to adopt the point of view of observing or witnessing.

Witnessing or observing does not focus on any idea or image, but allows them to flow by without involvement. One then realizes that the thought images are occurring spontaneously and the thought stream is impersonal. The thoughts are not "mine," as there is no "me" involved.

As the physical eye sees images, it does not claim authorship of the images, nor does the ear claim authorship of sound. Therefore, with some experience with witnessing and pure observing, it also becomes apparent that the thoughts are not authored by a unique personage called "I." They are the result of combinations and permutations of ideational and emotional programs that are playing on the game board. The realization that the mind is not the same as "I" or "me" breaks the identification of the self with the mind.

Nonresistance does not mean to ignore or deny. Instead, it means to witness, observe, and be aware—which, as an experiential style, moves one from being the imaginary actor in the movie of life to being the witness/observer, who is thereby emotionally uninvolved yet capable of participation. This attitude diminishes the temptation to invest in positionalities or outcomes. When personal will surrenders and Divine Will takes its place, Creation becomes continuous and evolutionary and subserves the unfolding of awareness.

There is no "who" witnessing, experiencing, or observing; rather, it is an innate quality that is operating effortlessly without the drain of the energy of intention to modify the process. All of life merely becomes a "given"—and awareness of the essence of subjectivity diminishes the sense of a personal "I" or "me" to the innate presence of the Self that is beyond thinkingness of content, but instead encompasses it. This awareness is the "Light" by which we "see" mentally and emotionally. By this awareness, focus now turns inward to the source of the Light, instead of to the details of what is illuminated. It is solely by this Light that one can even be aware of the content of mind, or else how would one even know what one is experiencing or thinking about?

Spiritual intention subserves, reinforces, and focuses on witnessing and observing rather than on "doingness" or specifics. Spiritual processing is like positioning oneself in the wind or in a water current.

The contemplative lifestyle facilitates transfer of the sense of identity from body/mind to witness/observer, which is more primary and closer to the Truth of the Self and Reality. The next step is the withdrawal of the sense of "I" from the witness/observer, where it moves to the faculty of consciousness/awareness itself, which is a quality rather than a personage. One major advantage of being the witness/observer instead of the participant is that the witness does not talk; it just sees without comment. It could be said that the witness/observer is aligned with the forest rather than the trees.

A useful decision or choice is to decide to stop mentally talking about everything and refrain from interjecting comments, opinions, preferences, and value statements. It is therefore a discipline to just watch without evaluating, investing worth in, editorializing, commenting, or having preferences about what is witnessed.

The witness/observer is a contemplative attitude of poise. Phenomena appear and disappear.

One must constantly surrender the desire to experience the phenomena or the desire to "juice" the experience of the experiencing itself.

※

Consciousness/awareness is located just beneath or prior to the function of the watcher/observer. It is silent and unmoving, like the sky or space itself. By relinquishing anticipation, clinging, seeking pleasure, or avoiding unpleasantness, the focus remains poised on the razor's edge of the crest of the fleeting moment. In this poised position, mental activity and imaging gradually recede, revealing that the underlying field is activated by the desire and intention of thinkingness itself.

As focus and interest move from content to the observer/witness, it will be found that the observer/witness is an emanation of consciousness as awareness—and a nonlinear, impersonal quality that is primary, innate, and autonomous.

※

Attention is selective based on presumptive value, which is only transitory. By watching what the mind selects for attention, its proclivities become apparent and reveal the sources of attraction and aversion. By relinquishment of the propensity to project either desire or aversion, all becomes of equal value when devoid of projected specialness.

One-pointedness of mind means to focus on the crest of the wave of witnessing/experiencing, plus being willing to surrender perceived loss or gain. That is the primary skill that is needed.

Spiritual evolution is the automatic consequence of watching the mind—and its proclivities as an "it"—from the general viewpoint of the paradigm of context rather than content. Instead of trying to force change, it is merely necessary to allow Divinity to do so by deeply surrendering all control, resistance, and illusions of gain or loss. It is not necessary to destroy or attack illusions but merely to allow them to fall away.

To watch the mind from a detached position is educational and nonstressful, and it can be done with equanimity.

With the style of detached observation, the unfolding of life reveals itself to be the consequence of the spontaneous emergence of actuality as a manifestation of potentiality when conditions are favorable.

6

MEDITATION

A specialized approach to transcending the self is meditation. Dr. Hawkins notes that the limitation of closed-eye sitting meditation is that it takes you out of the world, tending to polarize your spiritual work with your daily life (as you are either doing one or the other). Despite this noteworthy limitation, meditation provides spiritual students at various levels a means of disciplining the mind on their path to transcending it.

The purpose of meditation is to transcend the mind and its mental activities and limited perceptions, thereby transcending duality and becoming increasingly aware of Oneness.

To transcend level 600 (the emerging level of Enlightenment on the Map of Consciousness) requires dropping one's identification with the witnessing/observing qualities, which are actually autonomous qualities inherent to consciousness itself. With deep meditation, it is discovered that these qualities have unconsciously been identified with, which requires the surrender of the illusion or payoff of being the witness or the observer.

Witnessing and observing are autonomous, leading to the discovery that there is no actual "person" doing the witnessing and observing.

The intent of meditation is detachment, especially detachment from the notion that thoughts are "mine" or represent "me." In Reality, they are merely "its," as is the mind itself. The idea of ownership arises from the personalization of these thoughts due to familiarity because the mind (like a camera) was present to record these past thoughts, events, and memories. However, it recorded them only because they were imbued with importance. Note that little roadside detail is recalled from a boring cross-country drive. The mind's inner camera records what is valued. What was considered unimportant was not recorded.

Recall and rerun are also the consequence of imagined, projected value. Basically, with examination, it will turn out that the only real value is that something is "mine." Thus, just an ordinary shoe is not really noticed, but "my shoe" is now imbued with value and is therefore remembered.

Ninety-nine percent of the mind is already silent and without linear content. Only one percent is active (as proven by consciousness-calibration research), but that one percent is the focus of attention. Note by close observation that each thought arises from a silent, clear field of energy that is the source of thinkingness, ideas, and images. It does not arise, as the mind presumes, as a result of linear causation. On the contrary: each thought arises independently of all the others, like flying fish soaring out of the ocean. The ocean is like the silent, primary, *a priori* condition of the mind and thoughts. The concept that they are somehow caused or meaningfully correlated is actually a superimposed afterthought. Each flying fish arises independently of the others out of a primordial stillness.

One benefit of meditation is the discovery that, intrinsically, the energy field of the mind is itself basically void of thoughts, feelings, and images—and these activities actually occupy only about one percent of the total mind field. Like the sea beneath the waves, 99 percent of the mind is still, silent, and void; this can be detected and intuited if such a fact is made known to the student.

The undisciplined mind is attracted and glamorized by the active content of mind—with its kaleidoscopic parade of thoughts, images, and feelings—because of the subtle narcissistic payoff of these activities. To silence the mind, it is necessary to notice the subtle yet continuous payoffs, be willing to surrender these illusory gains, and instead identify with the mind as a silent energy field that is not limited to the personal self. Note that the ego is addicted to mentalization and craves its constant entertainment and stimulation, even if it includes negativity.

⁓⁓⁓

Q: How can meditation persist in one's daily existence?

A: By merely constantly posing the question to oneself of "what" is doing the acting, talking, feeling, thinking, or observing. This is a focus of attention with no languaging.

⁓⁓⁓

There is an energy in the mind that is constantly creating a stream of thoughts. You watch what is going through consciousness, like goldfish through a bowl. The thoughts are the goldfish, but *you* are the water. The unenlightened person thinks, *I am the goldfish; I am my thoughts; I am this worry; I am this fear; I am this regret.* You begin to identify where consciousness is. Consciousness is what is witnessing these thoughts. Thoughts are flowing through consciousness, and consciousness itself is invisible and has no form. You begin to identify with the observer instead of that which is observed.

To bypass and transcend the seductive attraction of the content of stream-of-consciousness thinkingness, humility about its importance quickly reveals the following: that without the projection of value, 99 percent of thoughts are just plain boring and platitudinous. Disenchantment with them diminishes their attraction by withdrawal of interest. The other illusion is that attention to thoughts is necessary to survival, whereas in reality, survival is up to the Self.

With sharp focus, it becomes apparent that thoughts can be relinquished earlier and earlier in the process of their emergence and formation. With continued focus and relinquishment of their entertainment value, they will slowly disappear as recognizable forms and subside to just being a transitory urge to think. The gratification of this impulse can be refused. By doing so, it becomes amazingly apparent that one thinks only as a consequence of desiring to do so, and that thoughts and images only have imaginary value.

The discovery that one is really the source of thinkingness reveals that one is not really the victim of the mind, but rather the originator of the phenomenon by virtue of intention and desire.

Freedom is a consequence of the deep humility that reveals that the only reason one thinks is because one wants to, in order to derive an experiential benefit or payoff.

It is simple to observe that although there is a "talking mind" going on at the same time, there is also a silent awareness that is more global and unfocused and operates automatically. Contemplation or meditation that focuses attention on context rather than content facilitates moving one's identity from the transient and volitional (thereby becoming personal) to the unchanging quality of awareness itself. This leads to the discovery that one is the field and not the specifics of the content. This jump in realization can be very sudden, which is a level of the Buddhist state of *satori*.

7

DEVOTION TO GOD
AND TRUTH

The devotional pathway, or the way of the heart, is another approach spiritual students can embrace. More than just religious observance, the devotional path requires the aspirant to surrender all of the self's proclivities to that which is greater—to the Truth of Divinity itself. His or her way of being then becomes love: a love for Truth and God and a willingness to let go and surrender anything blocking the experience of this love.

The ego often seems to collapse in a piece-meal fashion. Once faith in the reality of the ego as being the true self is undermined, its dissolution has already begun. When one's loyalty and allegiance is shifted from the ego to the ultimate reality of God, a space is created. Into the opening flows God's Grace, as represented by the Holy Spirit.

To strive to know God is in itself pristine and the ultimate aspiration.

A useful approach is to let the love for God replace the willfulness that is driving the seeking. One can release all desire to seek, realizing that the thought that there is anything else but God is a baseless vanity. This is the same vanity that claims authorship for one's experiences, thoughts, and actions. With reflection, it can be seen that both the body and the mind are the result of the innumerable conditions of the universe, and that one is at best the witness of this concordance.

Out of an unrestricted love for God arises the willingness to surrender all motives, except to serve God completely. To be the servant of God becomes one's goal rather than enlightenment. To be a perfect channel for God's love is to surrender completely and eliminate the goal-seeking of the spiritual ego. Joy itself becomes the initiator of further spiritual work.

In the end, it will be found that the sacrifice of letting go of the mind is actually the greatest gift one can receive.

If, in the exact passing moment of each instant, there is a complete willingness to totally surrender to it, one can suddenly transcend the ego in a flash. And then the way opens for Realization, wherein the Light of God as Self reveals the Source of all Existence and Reality.

If the ego has neither past, present, nor future to focus on, it falls silent and is replaced by the silence of the Presence. Thus, the way to sudden enlightenment is available at all times. It occurs naturally when the fascination with the story of the "me" of the past, present, or future is relinquished. The illusion of "now" is replaced by the reality of "Always."

The spiritual student is often seeking to transform, overcome, or slay the ego, when all that is necessary is to simply abandon it. This requires the development of trust, faith, and confidence in the Reality of God. When the seeking for gain is abandoned, life becomes relatively effortless and peaceful.

The mind of the aspirant has to bypass and refuse temptation. Later it will be seen that nothing was lost, as that temptation was merely another illusion. The aspirant gives up the vanities of opinionation and the duties of saving the world. One's inner spiritual evolution is of greater value to society than any form of doingness. The level of compassion radiates out and contributes silently to mankind's wisdom.

Without belief in its appearance as defined by perception, the world we thought was real disappears. When we choose to be at one with the inner, ever-present potentiality of joy and peace, the world transforms into a humorous amusement park—and all the drama is seen to be just drama.

The ego—or more accurately, the belief that one *is* the ego—obscures the Realization of the Reality of the Self as the Oneness of All That Is. The dissolution of the ego results in liberation from the bondage of the illusions that create suffering. These illusions are susceptible to fearless scrutiny that reveals the underlying fallacies. The only tool needed is the willingness to unreservedly surrender all beliefs, opinions, and attitudes to God.

The core of the ego is narcissistic pride; secretly, it thinks that it *is* God. Without undue strain, it can be caught in its secret, inflationary, dualistic presumptions, which are undone by simple humility. This is the doorway to freedom and the experience of happiness.

Negativity is based on an energetic *force* (of animal origin) that can be overcome only by *power*, which is solely of Divine origin. Therefore, it is operationally necessary to request and invoke God's help by whatever means available.

The real Self brings up the false self for investigation, which eventually leads to the disassembly of the ego structure itself. In the beginning, a seeker assumes there is a personal self that is seeking the real Self. Actually, it is the real Self that is drawing the seeker to it.

The ego equates survival of life with control. In a final surrender of control, the underlying primordial fear arises. Life is a consequence of the Divinity of its Source, which is the ultimate confrontation to the very core of the ego.

When peace is more valued than the entertainment of the insatiable ego, it will be discovered to be ever present and available. That one even has such an option is unknown by 99.7 percent of the population. Thus, there is an unknown freedom available: one can choose merely to refuse the ego investment in the world and one's thoughts about it (that is, surrender it to God).

To undo the grip of the mind requires a radical humility and an intense willingness to surrender its underlying motivations. This willingness receives energy and power from another willingness—the one that arises from the love of God—and the passion for surrendering love of thought for love of God.

To know what is necessary to reach Divine states accelerates progress; otherwise, there is an unconscious resistance of fear due to ignorance. This fear is overcome by the acquisition of the necessary understanding; therefore, there is nothing left to fear, and all fear is an illusion. This knowingness is also required at very advanced states.

One basic truth that is of inestimable value and usefulness is this dictum: all fear is fallacious and not based on fact. Fear is overcome by walking directly through it until one breaks through into the joy that the fear is blocking. The joy that follows facing any spiritual fear comes from the discovery that it was merely an illusion without basis or reality.

All descriptions, no matter how elegant, are nothing more than perceptual measurements and definitions of imputed qualities that have no self-existence. *Nothing is as it can be described;* therefore, all descriptions are of what a thing is not.

The realization of Absolute Reality and Truth is the greatest gift that one can be to the world and all humanity. Spiritual work, in its essence, is therefore a selfless service and surrender to the Will of God. As one's awareness increases, the power of that field of consciousness increases exponentially—and that, in and of itself, accomplishes more than all effort or attempts at relieving the suffering of the world. All such efforts are futile because they are necessarily misguided by the falsifications and illusions of the perceptual function of the ego itself.

"Mind" cannot be transcended by pursuing it, but only by the surrender of the illusion of mind as savior.

One can surrender the desire of thinkingness to God, which then quickly brings up the mind's fear of survival. At that point, one has to surrender the will to survive to God. If one stops thinking, there is the fear of being mindless. To be thoughtless is called "Divine idiocy," or "Divine stupidity." However, what actually needs to be known will reveal itself—not as thoughts, but as comprehension, understanding, and apperception via totalities.

The Infinite Reality is omniscient and independent of talkingness, thinkingness, and verbalization of words. The narcissistic ego is addicted to talkingness. It is of no value to the Self. The ego/mind believes that if it stops thinking/feeling, the personal self will die, for it is intrinsic to the ego's survival system. Therefore, it fears and avoids silence and stillness. The ego/self identifies with that which is linear, discrete, separate, and definable; that is, content.

Everyone already at a certain level knows that they "are"—the ego then quibbles about the details of definition, but the Self is not fooled by the ruse. All false identifications can be dropped in an instant with the willingness to surrender all mental activities to God.

Traditionally, the pathways to God have been through the heart (love, devotion, selfless service, surrender, worship, and adoration) or through the mind (*Advaita*, or the pathway of nonduality). Each way may seem more comfortable at one stage or another, or they alternate in emphasis. Nevertheless, it is a hindrance to consider that there is a personal self or an "I" or an ego that is doing the striving or seeking, or that will become enlightened. It is much easier to realize there is no such thing as the ego or an "I" identity that is doing any seeking; instead, it is an impersonal aspect of consciousness that is doing the exploring and seeking.

The attachment to the "I" core of the ego is the belief that it is the source of one's life, so surrendering it seems as though one is surrendering life itself to God.

Questions arise as to the source of the capacity to even realize Existence or Beingness, and whether such qualities are innate or are superimpositions by silent paradigm presumptions. One asks, "By what quality does the abstract even become discernible, and is not that knowingness itself merely a higher level of abstraction?" Again, although these queries may seem academic to the intellect, experientially, they are a priority and profoundly transformative as the light of the levels of consciousness. At the highest levels, they represent the last clouds that hide the radiance of the sun of Divinity.

～～～

There is no inner "thinker" behind thoughts, no "doer" behind actions, no "seeker" of enlightenment. Seeking occurs on its own when the time is right, and it emerges as a focus of attention. All aspects and qualities of consciousness are self-actuating and energize each other under the general direction of the will.

～～～

In Reality, everything is spontaneously manifesting the inherent destiny of its essence; it doesn't need any external help to do this. With humility, one can relinquish the ego's self-appointed role as savior of the world and surrender it straight to God. The world that the ego pictures is a projection of its own illusions and arbitrary positionalities. No such world exists.

～～～

Value, from the ego's viewpoint, is an emotionalized mentalization, and Reality does not require mentalization. With humility, one can

honestly state and witness that everything merely "is as it is," independent of projected worth.
Its intrinsic "value" is that it "is"; thusly, existence is complete within itself and is not needful
of projected nominalization as "special." When
the Divine Essence of All of Creation shines forth
without obstruction, then the ego/mind goes silent
in awe.

The basic purpose of spiritual work and dedication is to transcend the innate evolutionary
limitations of the ego and thereby access and
develop the nascent capacity of consciousness
itself, which bypasses all the limitations of the
ego/self. Truth then presents itself by virtue of
Divine Grace. Divinity reveals Itself to those who
call upon It in God's time. The pace of spiritual
evolution can seem slow, but spiritual endeavor
is never futile. Progress can become very sudden
and very major in dimension and impact.

Be passionate for God, not for belief systems.
That is the only real decision that has to be made
and can be applied to any and all situations. The

question is always whether to be at the effect of the world or aligned with the Truth of God instead. The search for enlightenment is different from that of seeking worldly success.

It is necessary to develop respect for spiritual endeavor. Straight and narrow is the path; waste no time or effort. Precision is discipline that is innate to serious commitment. Some students may yet be in a period of exploration, but once one gets the "fire in the belly," the urge to reach God becomes a relentless drive—or even, in the eyes of the world, a "madness." From that point on, there is no patience for amusement or diversion. It depends on decision, will, the level of consciousness, and karmic propensities. As it gets more intense, the love for and of God allows no delay.

All the truth that is necessary to know has already been spoken by actual beings on this planet. All Great Teachers proclaim the same truth, for there is none other. The Radiance of the Self within beckons one on and provides spiritual inspiration and strength. The Presence of God within is the source of one's existence; therefore, to seek one's source is in accord with God's Will.

⁘

One's commitment should be to God and Truth only. Teachers are to be respected, but devotion should be restricted to the Truth. As Buddha said, "Put no head above your own," meaning that one's only true guru is the Self (the Buddha nature).

⁘

The option for truth, peace, and joy is always available—although it's seemingly buried behind an ignorance and non-awareness that results from having chosen other options as a habit of thought. The inner truth reveals itself when all other options are refused by surrender to God.

⁘　⁘　⁘

Part III

REALIZING THE SELF

As Dr. Hawkins explains, the Reality of the Self is ineffable—beyond the limitations of mental activity, words, and concepts. The gift of the sage, however, is to approximate a description of the ineffable with a profound elegance and clarity that affords the spiritual student a glimpse of Ultimate Reality.

8

NATURE OF DIVINITY/ SELF/TRUTH

Different terms are used to describe Ultimate Reality. With energy fields vibrating at the highest levels expressible in the physical domain on up to infinity, Ultimate Reality transcends dualistic under-standing. This chapter offers Dr. Hawkins's descrip-tions for the nonlinear, nondualistic nature of All That Is and its related qualities.

Everything merely exists as it was created—complete and perfect. Everything fulfills its purpose by merely being what it is. Everything is the fulfillment of its own essence and potentiality. The only "requirement" for anything that exists is to just *be*. Its destiny under the conditions of any given moment is already completely fulfilled. Therefore, that which it is represents the completion of all past possibility up to that very moment; everything is the way it is supposed to be.

As essence fulfills its potentiality, it is witnessed by a corresponding level of consciousness. In any nanosecond of observation, nothing is actually changing. What is changing are the position of the witness and the point of observation. Change is merely a process of sequential perception. Life can be pictured as a series of stop frames, like the flip books of childhood. This poses the conundrum: is it the world that is moving, or is it the mind?

That which is ultimate and eternal transcends both objectivity and subjectivity and is beyond awareness. It is referred to in the ancient spiritual literature as "the Supreme Spirit." Out of the Supreme arises all that is manifest and unmanifest;

all consciousness and awareness; all existence; All That Is; either form or nonform; all that is linear and all that is nonlinear; all that arises out of creation; all possibility and actuality. The Supreme is beyond existence or nonexistence; beyond beingness or is-ness; beyond all Gods, heavens, or spiritual forms; beyond all names or definitions; beyond all divinities and spiritual denotations. It is out of the Godhead that Divinity arises, and out of the Supreme arises the Godhead.

Because the ego deals in form and definition, it cannot comprehend the Self—which is beyond all form, but without form would not appear to exist. In Reality, there is neither subject nor object; therefore, there is no relationship to be explained.

There is absolutely nothing in ordinary human experience to compare with the joy of the Presence of the Love of God. No sacrifice is too great, nor effort too much, in order to realize that Presence.

The Self is the Presence expressed as existence, and out of that consciousness arises the sense of existence.

To understand the nature of God, it is necessary only to know the nature of love itself. To truly know love is to know and understand God, and to know God is to understand love.

The ultimate awareness and knowingness in the Presence of God is Peace. That Peace proclaims infinite safety and preservation with infinite protection. No suffering is even possible.

The radical Reality is that to understand the essence of anything is to know God.

In Reality, everything occurs on its own, with no exterior cause. Every thing and every event is a manifestation of the totality of All That Is, just as it is at any given moment. Once seen in its totality, everything is perfect at all times, and nothing needs an external cause to change it in any way. From the viewpoint of the ego's positionality and limited scope, the world seems to need endless fixing and correction. This illusion collapses as a vanity.

***

Like springtime, the promise of a new era in man's understanding of God is emerging. Now the level of consciousness of mankind is high enough to be able to recognize the truth of a God of Love instead of worshipping a punitive god of guilt and hate.

***

That which is Reality is beyond all form and yet intrinsic to it. Let form reveal its own nature—there is no need to seek it. The actual essence of form is formlessness, as paradoxical as that may sound.

***

Innate to the Presence is an infinite, timeless Knowingness that illuminates all possibility, beyond all opposites or causality. Revelation presents itself as self-explanatory and obvious, the essence of all truth. The totality and completeness of the Knowingness prevails beyond time and is therefore always present. One reflection of this is the capacity to comprehend the incomprehensible by its self-revelation of its essence. Therefore, all stands revealed. The unmanifest and the manifest are one and the same.

Truth is radical subjectivity. With the collapse of the illusions of duality—including the supposed "reality" of a separate "self"—there remains only the state of the Infinite "I," which is the manifestation of the Unmanifest as the Self.

There is no division between Creator and that which is created. All is self-creating as the manifestation of the mind of God. This great awareness characterizes the consciousness level of the 700s on the Map of Consciousness, where Self is All That Is. Because the universe is self-evolving and self-fulfilling, no intervention is necessary. All is in perfect balance and harmony.

The Ultimate Truth is beyond is-ness, being-ness, or any intransitive verb. Any attempt at Self-definition, such as "I Am That I Am" or "I Am" is redundant. The Ultimate Reality is beyond all names. "I" signifies the radical subjectivity of the state of Realization. It is in itself the complete statement of Reality.

The infinite power of Divinity radiates down through the levels of consciousness like sunlight in the forest. It sustains all life. When deprived of the power of Light, consciousness reverts to its temporary illusory substitute called "force." Force is limited, whereas power is unlimited. Therefore, the end is certain as force cannot stand against power; and without the infusion of power, force—by its very nature—expends and extinguishes itself.

With the expansion of knowledge to include the nonlinear nonduality of Reality, it will become stunningly apparent that the most profound radically scientific statement that is possible to make is, in fact, *Gloria in Excelsis Deo*.

When one realizes that one is the universe—complete and at one with All That Is, forever without end—no further suffering is possible.

⁓

Note that both God and all references to the Divine are capitalized, and that of all the possible pronouns, only "I" is capitalized. The individual "I" can only be aware of itself or its existence as a consequence of the greater Awareness. This is the innate quality of the Divine "I," which is its source and the focus of the spiritual search. As such, it is thus nonverbal and the source of experiencing, witnessing, and observing. By analogy, one comes to realize that one is the water and not the fish.

⁓

The Self is Self-aware beyond the senses. Divinity shines forth as a massive revelation. Its obviousness is stark and forceful as a radiance. Its essence is certainty and finality, totality and completeness. All searches have ended.

⁓

God is All Present, simultaneously as manifest and unmanifest, as void and Allness, as visible and invisible, as the potential and the actual, as the expressed and the unexpressed.

It is important to realize this: that which is of God brings peace, and that which is not of God brings fear.

The infinite potentiality of the manifest becomes the actuality of the manifest by the Will of God as Creation.

The Self is the awareness—its source, its completion, its totality, its fulfillment, and its essence. It is the Reality of Reality, the Oneness and Allness of Identity. It is the ultimate "I-ness" of consciousness itself as the manifestation of the unmanifest. Thus, only can the indescribable be described. Amen.

Complete surrender to God unveils the Truth. Nothing is hidden; only the ego is blind. Reality lies just beyond the mind. Out of the fear of becoming nothing, consciousness denies its only reality that it is everything—the infinite, everlasting Allness out of which existence itself arises.

When the self dissolves into the Self, it is experienced as a great expansion from limited, transitory, and vulnerable to immortal, infinite Allness that transcends all worlds and universes. As such, the Self is not subject to death or birth, as it exists beyond temporality. The obscurity of the Self was the result of merely misidentifying perception as representing all Reality.

The mercy of God is infinite and unconditional.

Life is spawned by the light of Divinity, which is the Ultimate Source of all existence. In this unfoldment, consciousness is the agent.

Life is the radiance of God made manifest, as the universe expressed through evolution. We are both the product and the witness of Creation as a continuous, eternal process.

The infinite glory, greatness, and power of God has been severely and grossly underestimated and not comprehended by man. With the replacement of the self by the Self, the power of omnipotence is known by virtue of the fact that the Infinite is one's source and reality. There is no limitation to God.

The source of all life and all form is, of necessity, greater than its manifestations—yet it is neither different from them nor separate to any degree. There is no conceptual artifact of separation between Creator and created. As scripture states, that which is, was, and always shall be.

God is the absolute subjectivity that underlies existence and the capacity for awareness. God is beyond all time, place, or human characteristics.

In contrast to the ego's perception of God, the Absolute Reality of the Self is the manifestation of God as the very core of one's existence. The love of the Presence is ultrapersonal and experienced as infinite peace, infinite security, and the safety of foreverness so that there is no imaginary "end" to fear. The God of the Presence imbues the joy of completion. Love is not a "quality" of God but is God's very essence.

Whether one linguistically considers God to be called "Rama," "Brahma," or "Allah" is really irrelevant—God is not limited by any positionality or ascribable qualities. Likewise, God is not subject to the duality of either/or, which would have to be the basis of any favoritism.

The true Self is invisible and has no characteristics by which it can be judged. It has no describable qualities, nor can it be the subject of any adjectives at all. The Self merely *is* and is beyond verbs, adverbs, and adjectives. It does not even "do" anything.

The love of God is absolute and unconditional. The sky does not "be" for some people and "not be" for others, nor does the sun shine on only a select few who have been arbitrarily chosen. God is complete and total.

Realization is not a "gain" or an accomplishment, nor is it something that is "given" as a reward for being good—these are all notions from childhood. God is immutable and cannot be manipulated into granting favors, or seduced by bargaining or adulation. Worship benefits the worshipper by reinforcing commitment and inspiration. God is still, silent, and unmoving.

To know that the Self is context and that, in contrast, the self is content is already a huge leap forward. The naïve seeker merely keeps reshuffling the content.

～～～

The source of all that exists is Divinity; thus, all that exists is already perfect. Without that perfection, nothing could exist. From the viewpoint of enlightenment, one might say that the linear is observed from the context of the nonlinear. To put it differently, existence is the manifestation of Divinity as form. In and of itself, the universe is therefore harmless. The viewpoint from enlightenment transcends the experiencer, the observer, the witness, and even awareness itself.

～～～

Truth is strength as an expression of integrity.

～～～

The constant awareness of one's existence as "I" is the ever-present expression of the innate Divinity of the Self. This is a universal, constant experience that is purely subjective, and of which no proof is possible or necessary. The "I" of the

Self is the expression of Divinity as Awareness, which is therefore beyond time and form. The truth of this identity is obscured by the duality created by perception and disappears when all positionalities are relinquished.

The Self is not conditional; it has no qualities and is not dependent or explicable. The Self has no duration, beginnings or endings, location, form, or limitations. It is the Radiance of the Self that illuminates existence, without which there would be no awareness. The Self is beyond process. All descriptions are inappropriate and inapplicable to the Self.

The Love and Power of God are one and the same.

God can only be known and not proven. Beyond subjectivity, no world exists. Without the Presence of God, nothing could be known or experienced, even including one's own existence. Existence as subjectivity is complete, total, and whole; it is also the very basis of joy. The Self is the Presence of the Source of Existence as the Infinite "I."

The spontaneity of life is an expression of essences interacting effortlessly. The miracle of Creation is continuous, and all life shares in the Divinity of its Source, for nothing comes into existence except by Divine ordinance. Once the sacredness of life is revealed, there follows the knowingness of what is meant by the phrase *Gloria in Excelsis Deo!*

The concept of God doing battle with the forces of evil is an impossibility created by guilt-ridden, fearful fantasies. In Reality, there is no possible threat to heaven or to God or to the purity of Absolute Reality. The Real exists and the unreal does not, and the Real is not threatened by the unreal.

Life itself is not subject to cessation, but only to change of form. The Source and essence of life is God, Who is not subject to demise. One cannot lose one's source. Death is the end of one chapter of a series of stories that finally cease only when the ego-author surrenders to its source.

The Self is like one's inner grandmother who watches over a child so he does not forget to take his raincoat or mail the rent check. God is not ominous but loving; fear arises from the imagination.

The Presence of the Self is complete, permanent, and totally fulfilling—it has no needs. Everything occurs spontaneously as an expression of its intrinsic essence. There is nothing and no one to "cause" anything to happen.

The Infinite Supreme is the same for all mankind throughout all time. The God of all human religions is one and the same, and transcends all the tribal gods of old. God is both transcendent and immanent, both in heaven and within us. The realized Self is the knowingness of God Immanent, which is in accord with Christ's teaching that heaven is within us. The infinite, timeless Reality has also been historically referred to as the "Buddha Nature," "Christ Consciousness," the "Supreme" of Krishna, and so on.

Truth stands revealed on its own without proclamation or need of aggrandizement. Its Absolute Sovereignty shines forth without need of acclaim or praise.

The Self is beyond, yet innate in, all form— timeless, without beginning or end, changeless, permanent, and immortal. Out of it arises awareness, consciousness, and an infinite condition of "at home-ness." It is the ultimate subjectivity from which everyone's sense of "I" arises. The Infinite Reality does not even know itself as "I" but as the very substrate of the capacity for such a statement. It is invisible and all-present.

The source of the Self is the reality of Divinity. Although it is the source of existence, it is not subject to it, nor is such a term applicable.

The innate qualities of Divinity are mercy and compassion. There are no favors to be sought; it is only necessary to accept that which already exists as a given.

Divinity is without parts or division.

All that is truly of God brings peace, harmony, and love and is devoid of all forms of negativity. Spiritually aware persons realize that they can only carry the message, for it is the inner truth that is the teacher.

The Presence as Self illuminates the Allness of Reality. Everything is equal by virtue of the Divinity of its existence as the Infinite Supreme, out of which all existence and creation arise. There is no selectivity or division; all is of equal value and importance.

The purity of Divinity is beyond comprehension by the ego because the ego is limited by form and always assumes a duality of subject and object.

~~~~~

The universe is self-creating spontaneously. Nothing is causing it to express itself. The Unmanifest of the Godhead is the infinite potentiality of infinite context and all possibility. The universe is spontaneously autonomous—even the thought of "existence" is merely a notion.

~~~~~

God is the universal "I-ness" of manifestation. Behind even the universal "I-ness" of God is the Supreme as the Unmanifest, which is unnamable.

~~~~~

Because the essence of God is the catalyst of Creation, all that is created contains that same quality. Therefore, the ultimate context of God is an infinite progression of infinite potentialities and possibilities, each of which then creates a further infinite progression of infinite progressions.

Although not really satisfactory, the explanation is the view from the perspective of Self as at one with the Creator.

~~~

The Self knows, by virtue of its essence, all that exists beyond time and therefore beyond memory.

~~~

The Glory of God shines forth as the Source of Existence, as well as the Reality that is knowable by the subjective awareness of the Self as the Infinite "I."

~~~

The infinite context of all that exists and of all possibility is obviously God.

~~~

The possibility of the transformation from potentiality to actuality is provided by the infinite power of the primordial substrate of all existence, which alone has the power to transform the unmanifest into the realm of the manifest.

In Unity and Oneness, everything is simultaneously intrinsic to everything else, but not by virtue of being either the "same" or "else." Within the infinite context of Allness, potentiality is activated by Divine Ordinance, commonly known as God's Will. The term *will* is, however, somewhat misleading in that it implies volition. Creation is witnessed as the unfolding and revelation of the emergence of infinite potentiality as Creation. Thus, there is no duality of a "this" (Creator) creating a "that" (Creation), for Creator and Creation are one and the same.

Truth and Reality are identical and eternally present, merely awaiting discovery.

It is not possible to arrive at Truth and ignore consciousness, because Truth is the very product of consciousness.

The Presence of Self constitutes the classic *purusha,* or Radiance of Self as Source. Self "knows" by virtue of identity with Divinity itself. It thereby is its own Awareness, and by its Presence, it thereby makes itself "known" as the "Knower." Thus, it does not know "about," but is the completion of its own essence.

Divinity knows its own; therefore, to accept that truth is to already feel joy. To not experience joy by understanding this means that it is being resisted.

Enlightenment is not a condition to be obtained; it is merely a certainty to be surrendered to, for the Self is already one's Reality. It is the Self that is attracting one to spiritual information.

Because Divinity is nonlinear and intangible, God is the ultimate screen upon which to project the endless errors and proclivities of the human ego.

Consciousness-calibration research confirms that God is transcendent, inherent, and present in all that exists as the very Source of Existence itself. Thus, the nonlinear is simultaneously present in the linear.

The Self knows the Ultimate Reality by virtue of identity; it is it. The Self thereby recognizes the Presence.

The Allness of Divinity is strongly confirmed by the immense power of Love as intrinsic to Creation and Divinity. The Presence of Love is all-pervasive and experienced as one's intrinsic Self. It melts linearity into Oneness, which is simultaneously exquisitely gentle and—paradoxically—infinitely powerful. Love is the Ultimate Law of the Universe.

Divinity is the Source of all Existence, including one's own.

Q: *It is said that the seeker and the sought are one and the same. Is that correct?*

A: It is actually incorrect. That which is looking for the Self is the ego/self; thus, they are not the same. The Self has no need or capacity to search for that which it already is.

Realize that the depiction of God as a "judge" is an illusion of the ego that arises as a projection of guilt from the punishment of childhood. Realize that God is not a parent.

God's grace could be understood as the absolute certainty of the karmic coherence of the entire universe in all its expressions as realms and possibilities. Grace is the provision within the realm of consciousness for the availability to use all the means to salvation and absolute freedom. By choice, one determines one's own fate. There are no arbitrary forces to be reckoned with.

149

What is searching for higher truth is not a personal "I." Rather, it is an aspect of consciousness itself that expresses as inspiration, devotion, dedication, and perseverance—all of which are aspects of the spiritual will. Therefore, the source of the search for the Self is the Self itself actualizing the necessary processes by virtue of its own qualities, which are facilitated by Grace.

As can be discerned by consciousness research at this time, the infinite potentiality of the unmanifest became manifest as the energetic submatrix of the potential physical universe. In its contact with matter, the energy of consciousness actualized the potential of biological life. Consciousness as life is one and the same basic reality. In spiritual terminology, consciousness is the radiance of Divinity ("the light of God" of Genesis). Because the terms *God* or *Divinity* are problematic, in their place one can refer to Deity as "the ultimate omnipotent reality"—the absolute, irreducible Source of All Existence.

Subjectivity—devoid of content and beyond the duality of subject and object—is the Self. The subjective "I" of the Self is independent of content or form, beyond all thought or concepts. It is not feelings or thoughts that are important, but only the subjectivity that underlies their seeming importance.

Paradoxically, it is radical subjectivity that leads to the amazing discovery of the only possible true "objectivity." The only fact that can be objectively verified in all times and places and under all conditions by anyone anywhere is the absolute, irreducible fact of subjectivity.

Even radical scientific inquiry leads to the discovery that without subjectivity, nothing is knowable—nor could it even be said to exist. The awareness of awareness, the awareness of being conscious, and the awareness of content all depend on rising out of this subjectivity.

The subjectivity of consciousness is the illumination of the Self as the universal "I" of Reality. It is the Eye of God. That "I" is the Essence of All That Is and includes the totality of the Presence as the ever-present Source of Existence, beyond all time or place. It has no beginning and no end. Creation and the Creator are one and the same. To describe God as Manifest or

Unmanifest, or as transcendent or immanent, are only arbitrary points of view. Reality is beyond all such attempts at description.

Truth is autonomously self-evident by virtue of its existence as Allness.

Life, like existence, has no opposites—just as truth has no opposite, self-existent pseudo-reality such as falsehood. Truth is either present or not. Divinity, God, Allness, Oneness, and the Absolute are All That Is; no opposite to God can exist. Only the truth is true; nothing else exists. All fear, then, arises from attachment to form due to the illusion that form is a necessary requirement for existence.

Death is not possible to life any more than a shadow can kill light. Truth is not impaired or negated by falsity, and only its expression can be misunderstood or misrepresented. There is no opposite to life, to God, to Truth, or to the Allness of Reality.

The realization and knowingness of God is radically and purely subjective. There is not even the hypothetical possibility that reason could arrive at Truth. Truth is knowable only by virtue of the identity of being it.

Truth is the radical simplicity and obviousness of God. It is unity. The word *unity* signifies the completeness of the Self-identity of existence. All is complete by virtue of being itself. No descriptions or nominal designations are required; they are all distractions. Even to just witness requires no thought. There is no necessity to mentalize Reality; it does not enhance what *is* but instead detracts from it.

Evil is not the opposite of God but simply the denial of God, just as falsity is not the opposite of truth but its refusal.

Truth has no trappings. Many false teachers indulge in theatrical self-presentations that are merely lures and self-gratifications of being "special."

Truth is actuality; nontruth is false because it never existed and therefore was never recorded, which is why it exhibits a "false" (absence of truth) response to consciousness-research testing. Consciousness only responds to what "is" or "has been" in Reality. The source of consciousness is the Absolute Reality, classically called Truth.

The only energy that has more power than the strength of the collective ego is that of Spiritual Truth.

Truth reveals itself by virtue of the omniscience of the field of consciousness, in which omniscience recognizes the reality of Truth and does not give recognition to falsity—which is properly defined not as the opposite of truth, but as its absence.

The power of Truth itself is a quality of Divine Love that, in its infinite mercy, dissolves positionalities back into the Reality of the Self.

Proselytization is an expression of the vanity of the ego that seeks status through agreement or dominance. Truth is complete and total within itself and is therefore without needs.

Falsity is not the opposite of truth, but merely its absence. In reality, truth has no opposite, just as cold is not the opposite of heat, nor is light the opposite of darkness. (Darkness represents the absence of light, just as cold indicates the absence of heat.)

In reality, the Love of God, like the sun, shines equally on all.

The Ultimate is the realm of nonform, non-limitation, and nonlocality; therefore, it is the realm of the totality of the ever-present All.

~~~~~

There is only Existence. Existence requires no cause, and to think as much is to create a fallacy of logic. By Existence, we mean discernible through observation, and it imputes a hypothetical change of condition from nonexistent to existent. However, that which is *always* was in its completeness beyond all time; looking for a "primary cause" is an artifact of mental activity that arises along with the concepts of time and space. Beyond time and space, there are no events, no beginnings, and no endings that are beyond the categories of human thought or reason.

~~~~~ ~~~~~ ~~~~~

≈ 9 ≈

The Presence of God

One might say the "goal" of spiritual work is the discovery of the Presence of God, not as a transcendent "out there" entity, but as a radically subjective experience of Divinity within as well as without. Here, Dr. Hawkins provides direction, inspiration, and clarification to support this Realization.

The first evidence of the Presence of God is an awakening curiosity or interest in spiritual matters. That is the crack in the ego's dam. When the person begins to desire or practice spiritual goals or pursue spiritual information, the Presence is already taking hold of his life.

The experience of the Presence of God is available and within at all times, but it awaits choice. That choice is made only by surrendering everything other than peace and love to God. In return, the Divinity of the Self is autonomously revealed as ever present but not experienced— that's because it has been ignored or forgotten, or one has chosen otherwise.

Because mankind is an actualization of a potential by its Source, that Source is ever present and directly knowable as the subjective essence of the Self. The experience of the Presence as Self is transformative—and it is also identical throughout history, as reported by the sages of widely divergent cultures. The gift of Divinity is the potentiality within man's own consciousness

to return via that consciousness to the very
Source of his existence. With the realization of
the Self (the infinite context), the field and the
content merge into the reality of the Oneness of
the Source itself.

The totality of the Oneness of the All cannot
be "experienced." Instead, it is known by virtue
of being it. The "I" of the Self is the Eye of God
witnessing the unfolding of Creation as Now. Sequence is an illusion created by the perception of
the "I" of the ego, which is the point of observation of the processing of the nonlocal to the local,
of the nonlinear to the linear, of Allness to "this-
ness." Perception is the eye of the ego—which, as
it translates the unexperienceable Infinite to the
experienceable finite, produces the perception of
time, place, duration, dimension, position, form,
limitation, and singularity.

The discovery of the Presence of God is not
due to fear, but to the surrender that was precipi-
tated by the fear.

With the cessation of time, the doors swing open to an eternity of joy; the Love of God becomes the Reality of the Presence. The Knowingness of the Truth of all Life and Existence stands forth with stunning Self-revelation. The wonderment of God is so all-encompassing and enormous that it surpasses all possible imagination. To be at last truly and finally home is profound in the totality of its completeness.

The Presence of God is the quintessence of profound peace, stillness, and love. It is overwhelming in its profundity. It is totally enveloping, and the love is so powerful that it dissolves any remaining "non-love" held by the residual ego.

The infinite presence of all things is beyond all time and space, forever complete, perfect, and whole. All points of observation disappear, and there is the omnipresence of that which Knows All by the fact that it Is All. As Reality stands forth in its stunning self-evidence and infinite peace, it appears that the block to Realization was the mind itself, which is not different from the ego—they are one and the same.

In the Presence of God, all suffering ceases. One has returned to one's Source, which is not different from one's own Self. It is as though one had forgotten, or is now awakened from, a dream. All fears are revealed to be groundless; all worries are foolish imaginings. There is no future to fear, nor past to regret. There is no errant ego/self to admonish or correct. There is nothing that needs changing or improving. There is nothing about which to feel ashamed or guilty. There is no "other" from which one can be separated. No loss is possible. Nothing needs to be done, no effort is required, and one is free from the endless tug of desire and want.

The term *Self* emphasizes that God is discovered within as the Ultimate Reality that underlies one's actual existence in the "here and now" (to quote the Bible: "The Kingdom of God is within you").

Q: *What is the subjective experience or realization of Allness like?*

A: It is an awareness of a condition that has always been present. The novelty of sequential experiencing disappears—as do expectation, regret, or the desire to anticipate or control. Existence *as* Existence is total and complete. All one's needs are already fulfilled. There is nothing to gain or lose, and everything is of equal value. It would be like all movies being equally enjoyable because the pleasure stems from "going to the movies," and the movie that is playing is irrelevant.

To surrender identification with that which was presumed to be "me" allows the Real Me to shine forth as the immanent quality of Divinity that is the source of the unencumbered reality of "I."

The sense of "I" is an identification and a knowingness that are qualities of the Inner

Presence, which enable the capacity to know the "I" as Self. Stripped of all pretenses, the inner sense of "I-ness" merely knows Itself without any content.

No concepts are possible in the Infinite Light of the glory of God. There is a profound peace, safety, and "at home-ness." Completion has finalized.

The prevalence of inner silence is the threshold of the dawning realization that everything is happening of itself and that nothing is causing anything; one becomes aware that such constructions are merely forms of mental entertainment.

One can realize the Self as the primordial, irreducible Reality from any starting point. It is not the starting point that is important, but the dedication to relentlessly pursuing it to its very roots. To unravel the nature of experience leads to one's Source. Any leg of the elephant leads to the elephant.

The infinite field of the Source of All Existence is a radiant effulgence that shines forth, and its consequences as Creation are forever unified. Creator and Creation are one.

The experience of Divinity within as Self, or God Immanent, is quite different from belief in God Transcendent. It is for this reason that the Buddha counseled against all depictions or nominalizations of God, because Enlightenment is a condition or state in which the Self-knowing is that of Identity. In this condition or state, there is no "this," such as self, with which to describe the Self. The condition or state is best described as "Self-effulgent," and in that state the Knowingness is its own Reality.

The ego/mind is a learned set of behaviors, and the ultimate goal is to transcend its programming and functioning by virtue of the power of the Radiance of the Self, which recontextualizes life benignly. The Presence of the Self is experienced as compassion for all of life in all its expressions, including its evolution as one's personal self. As a consequence, forgiveness replaces condemnation, which is a sign that it is now safe to proceed deeper into serious inner inventory without undue stress.

To be at one with phenomena, instead of separate from them, results in experiencing the aliveness and Allness of the Presence expressed as All That Exists. All that has existence is not just passively "there," but instead seemingly presents itself to awareness as a quality of its existence rather than as a volitional intention. Thus, the universe appears to be a gift of exquisite beauty and perfection that shines forth with the intrinsic Radiance of Divinity.

Eventually even the illusion of witness/observer dissolves into awareness/consciousness itself, which is discovered to be nonpersonal and autonomous. There is no longer the limitation of "cause and effect" or "change." The illusion of "time" also dissolves into the Allness of Divine

Concordance. There is neither attraction nor aversion to existence itself, for even the manifest is seen to be a consequence of discernment by consciousness as a concept.

The Realization of the Presence of Divinity unfolds of its own when the ego and its perceptual positionalities are surrendered.

The Peace of God experientially transcends all prior states, as exquisite as they might have been.

Divine Love is an all-inclusive field, and its quality is unforgettable, as anyone who has ever had a near-death experience knows. It is intrinsically truly ineffable, and its Presence is like a meltingness in its exquisite, experiential totality. There is nothing in worldly life that even comes close to it. It is profoundly gentle, yet infinitely powerful by virtue of its intrinsic infinite strength.

Innate to the Presence as Love is the quality of timelessness/foreverness. Even a brief moment of the Presence in earthly time is realized via the Self to be eternal. This is an unmistakable hallmark. Therefore, to have known the Real for even a few brief moments of clock time is to know it forever.

Divinity is Infinite Love. Within its Presence, even relinquishment of bodily existence is not a "problem" or a source of resistance . . . as the ego dissolves, so do all its fears and presumptions. The Inner Reality is immune to considerations or doubts. The Self is Certainty.

The Radiance of God is the light of awareness that reveals the Divinity of all that exists. In the stillness of the Infinite Presence, the mind is silent, as there is nothing that can be said; all speaks of itself with completeness and exactitude. With this realization, one transcends the final duality of existence versus nonexistence because only existence is possible. The opposite of Truth does not exist, since Reality excludes nonreality. In this realization resides the Peace of God.

Fear itself actually precludes the awareness of the Presence of God. Only when it is abandoned does profound surrender of the resistant ego reveal a peace beyond understanding.

There is nothing more wonderful than arriving back home again at one's Source. The illusion is that one struggles with spiritual growth by one's own effort; in fact, we are pulled into greater awareness by the Will of God expressed as the Holy Spirit, and all that is necessary is to allow it to happen by surrendering completely. For truly, only God is God.

10

NONDUALITY

The Reality of the Self is characterized as non-dual: beyond form and the duality of "this" and "that," subject and object, "mine" and "yours." The state of nonduality is generally described by highlighting what it is not, pointing to a reality that can't be accurately described, only subjectively experienced.

An analysis of the nature of consciousness reveals that redemption occurs as the result of the return of consciousness to its original pristine state of nonduality. It can do so only by the "obedience" of surrendering the dualities of will and willfulness of the ego to the nonduality of God's Truth. The return from the duality of the ego to the nonduality of the spirit is so difficult and unlikely that only by Divine Grace is it even possible. Thus, man needs a savior to be his advocate, his inspiration, and the fulcrum of his salvation from the pain and suffering of the ego.

Ego/mind *thinks*, field (consciousness) *knows*, and Self *is*.

Nonduality means without form, division, or limitation—such as time, locality, or mentalization—including arbitrary linear presumptions. Divinity is, by its innate "qualities," omniscience, omnipresence, and omnipotence; and all evolves as a consequence of the Unmanifest's becoming Manifest as evolutionary Creation.

In Reality, from a nondualistic viewpoint, it can be observed and experienced that everything is actually occurring spontaneously as the field effect of the automatic consequence of the manifesting of potentiality into actuality. Unseen is the underlying power of the infinite context of Consciousness/Reality/Divinity and its effect on content. The nonlinear, infinite field of power is equally present within, without, and beyond. Potentiality becomes actuality when conditions permit or are favorable. The process is empowered by intention, as well as by the innate impersonal quality of consciousness itself.

In the nonduality of awareness, even sequence no longer occurs, and awareness replaces experiencing. There is no longer the experience of "moments," as there is only a continuous Now. Movement appears as slow motion, as though suspended outside of time. Nothing is imperfect. Nothing actually moves or changes; no events actually take place. Instead of sequence, there is the observation that everything is in a stage of unfoldment, and that all form is only a transitional epiphenomenon created by perception and the observational habits of mental activity.

In Reality, all comes into being as an expression of the infinite potentiality of the universe. Evolving states are the consequences of conditions but are not caused by them. Conditions account for appearances, and the phenomenon as change is really the result of an arbitrary point of observation.

※

In the Reality of nonduality, there is neither privilege nor gain nor loss nor rank. Just like a cork in the sea, each spirit rises or falls in the sea of consciousness to its own level by virtue of its own choices—not by any external force or favor. Some are attracted by the light and some seek the darkness, but it all occurs of its own nature by virtue of Divine freedom and equality.

※

Inasmuch as the entire universe and everything in it is a karmic unity, the Allness of Reality is the realization of enlightenment. If all is a karmic unity that originates from the same source, then to see any separation is an artifact of perception. In Reality, the one and the many are the same.

The small self is dissolved by the Self. The healing attitude of the Self to the self is compassion; it is through forgiveness that one is forgiven. This willingness to surrender, arising out of the Grace of God, permits the power of God expressed as the Holy Spirit to recontextualize understanding—and, by this device, to undo the reign of perception and its attendant duality, which is the source of all suffering. The dissolution of duality is the ultimate gift of God, for it dissolves the very source and capacity for suffering. In nonduality, suffering is not possible.

On the level of nonduality, there is observing but no observer, as subject and object are one. You-and-I becomes the One Self experiencing all as Divine.

Within nonduality, positionality is not possible; thus, dualistic perceptions stemming from

positionalities are the source of the misunder-
standings about God for which, unfortunately,
mankind has paid a great price.

To transcend the linear to the nonlinear
is the way of the mystic—the pathway of nonduality—to realize the inner light of consciousness itself, the True Immortal Self. Everyone
trusts the inner sense of reality or capacity to
"know" that underlies all experiencing and witnessing, no matter what the content. The content of mind thinks, but only the nonlinear field
"knows," or how else would it be possible to know
what is being thought?

Because everyone actually lives in the experiential at every moment, the Source of the capacity to know or experience is close at hand and is
itself pristine. All human beings experience that
they are continuously "experiencing," no matter
what the ever-changing content might be.

All humans are already mystics and innately attracted to enlightenment, whether they
are aware of it or not. It is an extension of the

qualities of learning and curiosity, which are innate to the mind. Thus, the pathway of "Devotional Nonduality" is open to everyone and has no requirements, other than the capacity for inner honesty and the willingness to align with verifiable truth and follow it to its Source.

Q: Is nonduality like radical reality, in which everything is seen as the expression of its essence by virtue of its identity?

A: That is an essential insight. All Creation, in and of itself, moves from perfection to perfection solely by virtue of its existence. Existence is already the fulfillment of potentiality expressed as the actuality.

The knowingness that arises from within is innate, accessible, and experiential. Such knowingness is also beyond definition or description as the primary, confirmable, universal substrate of power and energy—out of which arises the possibility as well as actualization of existence. This Ultimate Reality is revealed via the search into the substrate and source of consciousness itself, which is the ultimate nonlinear context beyond all definition. Thus, via the pathway of enlightenment, there is no separate relationship of "you-God" vis-à-vis "me-human." This is the meaning of the *Advaita* (nonduality) terminology of Self as compared to self. This is the illuminated core of the mystic, by which the ultimate nonlinear Reality is self-revealing when the obstacles of the linear ego have been relinquished.

In Devotional Nonduality, the likelihood of error is bypassed by devotion to the essential nonlinear qualities of Divinity itself, such as compassion, oneness, love, truth, omniscience, eternal, infinite, omnipresence, and omnipotence—beyond form, place, time, human instincts, or emotions.

While the primary prerequisite for adherence to religion is faith, the essential required qualities needed for following the pathway of nonduality are humility, surrender, and devotional dedication to the pathway.

It is readily observable that followers of religions are characterized by the presumption of "I know" via scriptural authority, ecclesiastical doctrine, historical precedent, and so on. In contrast, the spiritual devotee for nonduality starts from the basic, more truthful position that "I, of myself, *don't know*."

Q: What is different about the pathway of Devotional Nonduality compared to traditional teachings?

A: It is characterized by the elimination of all trappings and nonessentials, for time is short and narrow are the gates. It is therefore not pertinent to the past; that is, to doctrine, dogma, historical rituals, personages, events, or belief systems. Empowerment is from within by assent of the will. Truth stands forth of its own when the obstacles are removed. The call is from within rather than a response to exhortation from without. The Source is both the initiator as well as the destination.

Spiritual information is now available for the first time that, throughout history, has never before been accessible. The capacity to identify truth from falsehood and the degree of its expression is now a major asset and advantage. According to consciousness research, the likelihood of reaching enlightenment is now approximately one thousand times more likely than it was in the past.

Q: *Is not the pathway of Devotional Nonduality arduous?*

A: It is not the pathway that is arduous, but merely the degree of the ego's resistance to it. This resistance is overcome by invoking the will—which then institutes the spiritual capacities for dedication, effort, and the willingness to surrender obstacles.

Devotion invites the power of love, by which humility removes the ego's props and positionalities. It also activates the utilization of information that is transformative. Intention energizes willingness, which thereby enables transformation to replace the limitations consequent to resistance.

To adopt the pathway of Devotional Nonduality recontextualizes the obligation to the pursuit of Truth rather than worldly involvement and action. How best to serve the world is concordant with comprehension.

Commitment is to the core of Truth itself, and it is free of seduction by proselytization or secrecies. All that is necessary is a curiosity and attraction to Truth—which is complete, total, and self-sufficient.

The "Infinite I" is that subjective reality that underlies the individual "I" and allows for the experience of "I-ness" as one's existence. It is the absolute "I" that enables the statement, "I." Consciousness, or the capacity for awareness, is formless and is the backdrop from which form can be identified.

Ultimate Truth is realized as pure, radical subjectivity. It is self-revealing and beyond argument.

The source of the highest Spiritual Truth is nonmental. The intellect has difficulty comprehending this critical fact because the mind is intrinsically dualistic and limited, expecting a "this" to come from a "that." In the advanced spiritual Reality, duality dissolves because the "this" *is* the "that." The seeker and the Sought become One with the transcendence of the limitation of duality; that is, Realization of the Self, Illumination, and Enlightenment.

A religion primarily addresses the realm of duality, whereas enlightenment addresses nonduality. This strict path to enlightenment says that inasmuch as duality is illusion, there is no point in trying to perfect it. Therefore, the ego is to be transcended and seen for the illusion that it is. "Good personhood" is laudable, but it does not of itself result in enlightenment. The possibility of reaching enlightenment is based on advanced understanding of the nature of consciousness itself.

When the conditions—including mind-set, intention, and dedication—are favorable, a decision may arise to drop everything in the world. One might then throw oneself totally into an all-out, "go for it," continuous, laser-like, focused surrendering of the perceiver/experiencer aspect of the ego. This process takes one quite rapidly beyond the mind to the very "processing edge" of the experiencer.

This "processor" edge is the actual locus of the ordinary sense of "I-ness," and it creates a 1/10,000th-of-a-second delay between reality (the world as it is; Descartes's *res extensa*) and the world as it is perceived or experienced (Descartes's *res cogitans*). This separation is the crux and locus of the self's illusion of duality, which obscures comprehension of the intrinsic Reality of Nonduality (Self). With transcendence of the illusion of a separate, individual, personal self, there emerges the Radiance and Oneness of the Self—by which all life, whether denoted as subjective or objective, is recontextualized into Oneness.

11

ENLIGHTENMENT

The human mind can wrestle to no avail for an understanding of enlightenment. As Dr. Hawkins points out: "In actuality, enlightenment is neither a state nor a viewpoint; yet it is both, and there is no statement about it that is completely accurate."

Often synonymous with Self-realization, enlightenment is the nondualistic state that begins to emerge at the level of consciousness denoted as Peace. Enlightenment isn't a goal to be obtained; it's a condition that manifests when the ego/mind is transcended. Enlightenment isn't an end in itself. Again, from Dr. Hawkins: "Enlightenment is a progressive realization and does not represent a finished product, or a final end, or the completion of the evolution of spiritual possibility."

Enlightenment is merely the emergence of Truth when the obstructions to the realization of that Truth have been removed. By analogy, the shining of the sun is not conditional upon the removal of the clouds; it merely becomes apparent.

The term *enlightenment* is semantically correct. It is the recognition and realization that one's reality is the light of the Self—and that it stems from within as an awareness and profound, self-evident Reality.

To even hear of enlightenment is already the rarest of gifts. Anyone who has ever heard of enlightenment will never be satisfied with anything else.

A "good person" is one thing; enlightenment is another. One is responsible for the effort and not the result, which is up to God and the universe.

One can spend endless lifetimes studying all the religious and philosophical teachings of the world and merely end up confused and discouraged. Seek to "know," not to "know about." "Know" implies subjective experience; "know about" means to accumulate facts. In the end, all facts disappear and there are none to be known. If one realizes that one's own Self is the All of Everything that is, has been, or ever could be, what is left that one needs to know? Completeness is, by its very nature, total and finished.

That which I am is Allness. To realize that one already is and always has been All That Is leaves nothing to be added.

The way to sudden enlightenment is through strict adherence to spiritual awareness and specifics of consciousness so that the personality (ego) is transcended rather than perfected.

In Reality, time is merely an illusion and an appearance. No "time" is really wasted once one has chosen the spiritual goal. Actually, it makes no difference in the end whether enlightenment takes a thousand lifetimes or one. In the end, it is all the same.

To understand the nature of consciousness makes enlightenment possible. This essentially entails the realization of the difference between duality and nonduality, as well as how to transcend the realm of duality.

The essence of man includes the potentiality for enlightenment. Readiness implies that one has evolved through the lower levels of consciousness, so spiritual inspiration now becomes the spark that ignites the quest.

From the viewpoint of consciousness and enlightenment, the reign of fear does not cease until the desire for existence itself is surrendered to God. In the silence that ensues comes a great realization that one's existence has always been due to the Presence of the Self, which has attracted from the Universe whatever is necessary for survival.

※

When one stops identifying with either the body or the mind, the functions continue autonomously, but merely without an identification as "myself." The sense of authorship disappears. Ongoing survival is autonomous, and continuance is an expression of consciousness in its alliance with the Holy Spirit.

※

Q: Is there no escape from the ego and its karma?

A: Enlightenment is the only total escape, and spiritual endeavor helps to loosen its hold.

※

Salvation requires purification of the ego; enlightenment requires its total dissolution. The goal of enlightenment is more demanding and radical.

Clarify that it is not a personal "you" who is seeking enlightenment, but an impersonal quality of consciousness that is the motivator.

Q: Can you summarize the critical element for the evolution of consciousness to the state of enlightenment?

A: Note that the ego habitually takes a positionality. In the naïve person, it is usually unspoken or unconscious. Positionality then automatically creates a duality of seeming opposites. At this point, the mind is creating the world of perception—which is like a lens that distorts, enlarges, or diminishes meaning and significance. This perception is the product of belief systems and presumptions and thus becomes a distracting filter. Therefore, essence cannot be perceived from a dualistic positionality.

Input is run through the software programs that simultaneously edit the incoming programs. Reality is consequently obscured and hidden behind a perceptual screen; therefore, the self lives in a perceived, edited translation of information.

This processing creates an extremely small time delay (estimated at 1/10,000th of a second). This editing function of perception simultaneously interprets meaning in which the intellect and especially the memory play significant roles.

There is no separation in the Allness of Creation, so it is impossible for the created to be separate from the Creator. Enlightenment is therefore the revelation of the Self when the illusion of the reality of a separate self is removed.

The seeking of enlightenment is a very major commitment—and is, in fact, the most difficult of all human pursuits. Enlightenment as the primary goal of one's life occurs in only one in ten million people.

The oneness of Self-identity is the substrate of the phenomenon known as Revelation or Realization. Enlightenment is the finalized state that ensues—and it is unconditional, total, and complete.

To be enlightened merely means that consciousness has realized its most inner, innate quality as nonlinear subjectivity and its capacity for awareness.

The personal "I" is "content," whereas the "I" of Reality is context. By analogy, the cloud is subject to change and dissolution. Weather comes and goes, but the sky itself remains unchanged. Enlightenment is merely the shift of identity from the cloud to the sky.

Be resolute on the level of absolutely no reservation. Avoid the lure of the astral realms. Beware of the wolves in sheep's clothing, for they are attracted to the devotee who is making significant progress. Do not accept anyone into your life who does not pass the calibratable level of Truth. Keep your spiritual goal ever in awareness, no matter what the activity. Dedicate all endeavors to God. Remember the true nature of God and avoid any teachings that state otherwise.

The desire to search for God or enlightenment is already evidence of having been spiritually inspired. As the ego vacates, the Radiance of
the Self uplifts and inspires. Henceforth, it is not
possible to be alone. At the critical moment, spiritual commitment and dedication bring forth the
unseen help of the Great Beings who are no longer in physical bodies—yet their energy stands at
the great doorway of the final moment when one
is sustained by the Holy Spirit and the wisdom of
the teachers of Truth.

It is important to realize that the destiny of
those who choose enlightenment is enlightenment—who else would be on such a quest? To
merely seek spiritual purification and awareness
is already a gift.

The straightest way to enlightenment is
through devoted introspection, meditation, and
contemplation of the inner workings of the ego
so as to understand consciousness. The process is

energized by intention, dedication, and devotion; and the total effort is supported by spiritual inspiration. The dedication is focused on the process itself as a surrender to God. The focus needs to be intense, and it is energized by fixity and deliberateness of intention. The process is one of discovery and becomes progressively self-revealing.

~~~

To follow the strict pathway to enlightenment is a specific discipline and commitment. It is not the same as practicing a religion. While there are many tenets of religion that support the search for enlightenment, there are also many that do not and actually constitute a hindrance. To be pious is one thing; to be enlightened is quite another.

~~~

Enlightenment means that the former personal identity and all that had been believed about it have been erased, removed, transcended, dissolved, and displaced. The particular has been replaced by the universal, qualities have been replaced by the nonlinear, and the discrete has been replaced by the unlimited.

When a devotee commits to the pathway of enlightenment, then the wheat has to be winnowed from the chaff. This is automatically so, because positionalities are based on beliefs. Beliefs disappear in the face of the knowingness of Truth.

The road to enlightenment is not for bleating sheep. To be offended signifies that one is defended, which, in itself, signifies the clinging to untruth. Truth needs no defense and therefore is not defensive; Truth has nothing to prove and is not vulnerable to being questioned for an answer.

When enlightenment occurs, the ensuing state also completely reconstructs the appearance of the world. Everything is seen to happen of its own. There is no longer a "me" or a personal "I." The orientation to the world is completely altered, and functioning may be impossible or very difficult.

Because no languaging of the state of en-lightenment is actually possible, a Zen master may just suddenly shout "Ha!" and hit you with a stick. What is hoped for is a sudden flash, during which the inexplicable Reality stands revealed.

In the state of enlightenment, all is self-revealing of its essence as its existence. Every-thing already is what it "means."

Enlightenment is the ultimate aesthetic awareness, for it allows the beauty of creation to shine forth with stunning clarity.

Another simple analogy is that a shadow does not become a sunbeam, but rather is replaced by it. The ego is the shade; enlightenment is the con-sequence of the light of the Self that replaces it.

The capacity to reach the condition or state classically called "Enlightenment" represents the fulfillment of the potential of consciousness in its evolutionary progression.

꒰꒱

Enlightenment is merely the full, conscious recognition that innate Truth is the core of one's own existence—and that God as Self is the illumination whereby that realization is made possible. The Infinite Power of God is the manifestation of the power of Infinite Context. The Unmanifest is even beyond Infinite Context.

꒰꒱

The straightest way to Enlightenment is by transcending the limitation of the ego/mind by dedication to verified Truth itself. This process is suitable for modern humankind and devoid of conflict with science and religion.

꒰꒱

As the Buddha pointed out, being mortal automatically entails suffering, which is why he taught to seek enlightenment in order to preclude that karmically determined recurrence. At very high levels, the subjective experiencing of existence is no longer limited by the narcissistic ego or the psychological blocks of the positionalities. This condition is the consequence of progressive surrendering at great depths of all limitations and belief systems. The requirement is the persistent "one-pointedness of mind," processing out the emotional/mental residuals of lower consciousness levels and surrendering all self-identities and mental belief systems.

Consistent application of any spiritual principle can unexpectedly result in a very major and sudden leap to unanticipated levels. At that point, memory may not even be available; instead, the Knowingness of Spiritual Truth presents itself silently.

Enlightenment is the consequence of the surrender of all dualistic illusions to Truth. All suffering ends with dissolution of the ego's positionalities. Thus do we praise the Lord God for radiating Light to the world.

Comfort and confidence can be derived from this verifiable reality: that the rare persons who are actually attracted to enlightenment as a life goal are attracted because that is already their destiny. For the same reason, only future golfers would be taking golf lessons.

To seek enlightenment is a major decision. The decision itself is therefore akin to a "yang" position—but subsequently, the process itself is more intrinsically akin to a "yin" posture. While the ordinary ego is programmed to "getting" (yang), spiritual intention now shifts to "allowing" (yin).

The dedication to Self-realization and enlightenment is a disciplined straight-and-narrow path. Thus, a serious devotee is advised to bypass the attraction of curiosity and appeal to the inner child offered by the magical and mysterious paranormal and psychic phenomena that are commonly merchandized and proffered as learn-able skills.

The state of enlightenment is therefore the potential Reality that replaces the illusions of the ego's perceptual positionalities. Spiritual inten-tion, effort, and decision potentiate the evolution of consciousness from the linear limited to the nonlinear Allness of Reality.

Enlightenment is the consequence of a major shift of content and identification. The experi-encer focus is like a screen that veils Reality and drops of its own accord when the props are re-moved. This is the consequence of surrendering the will to God. The sense of reality of the self was actually due solely to the underlying Pres-ence of the Self.

To seriously seek enlightenment is a very strict discipline that therefore eschews the attrac-tion of involvement in supposed spiritual move-ments that are actually intrinsically political in nature and factional. The attraction of "changing the world" (for the presumed better, of course) appeals to the naïve idealism of the inner spiritual adolescent and is transcended with maturity. The nature of human life is the automatic consequence of the overall level of human consciousness itself. Therefore, to benefit the world, it is necessary to change not the world but oneself—for what one becomes is influential by virtue of its essence (nonlinear) and not its actions (limited and linear).

Straight and narrow is the path, for without inner discipline, the spiritual energy becomes dissipated in diverse attractions.

The energy of life is a radiance from the field of consciousness, which is the mode of the Presence of Divinity that manifests in physicality as Creation. The capacity for enlightenment is merely a consequence of consciousness returning to its source, which is Divinity Immanent as Self.

The ego/self identifies with its various functions and qualities and labels them as "me" and says that is "who I am." This results in the vanity of authority, an error that originated during evolution as a consequence of identification with the experience of the senses. Thus comes about a typical conclusion that "I" itch, instead of "the body" itches. The same error of authorship/ownership occurs with feelings and thoughts in that the witness identifies with the subject and the content of the experiencer.

The experiencer function is an information probe that collects linear data and therefore is an "it" and not a "me." It is a functional processing unit similar to the senses of smell or touch.

The relinquishment of the ego's positionalities reduces its dominance and opens the door for comprehension and awareness that are nonlinear and nonconceptual. Thus emerges the "Knowingness" of the Self, by which conflicts spontaneously dissolve. These inner transformations are accompanied by quiet joy and relief, as well as a greater sense of internal freedom, safety, and peace. The power of Love of the Self progressively predominates and eventually eclipses all negative feelings, doubts, and obstacles.

Transformation is thus not experienced as the loss of the self, but rather as the gain of the emergence and unfoldment of the Self, which is of a much greater dimension. What actually emerges is a change of state or condition that supersedes and replaces the old. Thus, the lesser is replaced by the greater, by which spiritual evolution reveals the Presence of God as Immanent. This discovery is the change in the state of consciousness historically referred to as "Enlightenment" or "God-consciousness."

Note that the Self is the formless subjective source of the capacity for awareness. It is like the "hardware" of a computer—innocent, permanent, unchangeable, unlimited, timeless. On the other hand, the ego records and processes all data in the domain of form and constitutes the "software," which is an accumulation of programs. The average person identifies with the ego software programs as his identity: "me" or I. The condition of enlightenment is the replacement of the identification of self with the Self, the source of awareness itself. Thus, God is knowable and known as immanent (in here); whereas to the ego, God is seen as transcendent only (out there).

Awareness itself is beyond even consciousness. Therefore, it may be said that the Absolute is unknowable exactly because it is beyond knowing; that is, beyond the reach of consciousness itself. Those who have attained such a state of awareness report that it cannot be described and can have no meaning for anyone without the experience of that context. Nonetheless, this is the true state of Reality, universally and eternally; we merely fail to recognize it. Such a recognition is the essence of enlightenment, and the final resolution of the evolution of consciousness to the point of Self-transcendence. The Self replaces the self.

The goal of society in general is to succeed in the world, whereas the goal of enlightenment is to transcend beyond it.

It is helpful to remember that neither Truth nor enlightenment is something to be found, sought, acquired, gained, or possessed. That which is the Infinite Presence is always present, and its realization occurs of itself when the obstacles to that realization are removed. It is therefore not necessary to study the truth, but only to let go of that which is fallacious. Moving away the clouds does not cause the sun to shine but merely reveals that which was hidden all along.

Spiritual work, therefore, is primarily a letting go of that which is presumably known for that which is unknown—with the encouragement that the effort is more than well rewarded from others who have realized the Infinite Presence.

To best serve the world, seek enlightenment and transcend illusions rather than contribute to them.

Investigation into the nature of consciousness leads directly to the very source of illumination, for the Light of Consciousness is the condition of enlightenment. By its Light, the knower and the known are united in the realization of the Self as God Immanent.

Consciousness does not recognize separation, which is a limitation of perception. The enlightened state is a "Oneness" in which there is no division into parts. Such division is only apparent from a localized perception; it is only an accident of a point of view.

～

The Infinite, Ultimate Potentiality is the Actuality of Existence. "All That Is" is therefore innately Divine, or it could not exist at all. The absolute expression of Divinity is Subjectivity. If I exist, then God Is. Enlightenment is the verification that all existence is not only the result of Creation, but existence itself is not different from the Creator. The created and the Creator are one and the same.

～

Through spiritual alignment, intention, and devotion—aided by meditation, contemplation, authenticated instruction, and Truth; and assisted by the energy field of an advanced teacher—great leaps of consciousness can occur unexpectedly. Thus, it is important to know of these leaps well in advance, as confirmed by con-sciousness research.

The chances of becoming enlightened are now more than one thousand times greater than at any time in the past, which means that reach-ing the level of Unconditional Love (calibration 540) is a very attainable and practical goal. From the level of Unconditional Love, the pathway is increasingly joyful. At level 600, there occurs an infinite, silent stillness and peace—and progres-sion from there is up to the Will of God, karma, and the potentialized Knowingness nascent within the spiritual aura.

Truth is recognized. It presents itself to a field of awareness that has been prepared in order to allow the presentation to reveal itself. Truth and enlightenment are not acquired or achieved. They are states or conditions that present them-selves when the conditions are appropriate and the obstacles are removed.

All avenues of questioning lead to the same ultimate answer. The discovery that nothing is hidden and Truth stands everywhere revealed is the key to enlightenment about the simplest practical affairs and the destiny of mankind. In the process of examining our everyday lives, we can find that all our fears have been based on falsehood. The displacement of the false by the true is the essence of the healing of all things visible and invisible. And always, a final question will eventually arise for every questioner—the biggest question of all: "Who am I?"

❧

You have to let go of the illusion that you know who you are. In the Divine state, there is nothing to "know" about because you *are* it. That is a difficult leap to make—but suddenly, it occurs of its own accord, and then one is free forever. Uncertainty is replaced by endless delight. Human life is then an endless comedy! You're not a "who" but a "what."

❧

One reason for the seemingly endless delays on the way to enlightenment is doubt, which should be surrendered as a resistance. It is important to know that it is actually extremely rare for a human to be committed to Spiritual Truth to the degree of seriously seeking enlightenment, and those who do make the commitment do so because they are actually *destined* for enlightenment.

Who am I? Who is asking? You find out who is asking, and that answers the whole question. It's not a "who" but a "what."

<hr />

At the last doorway to enlightenment stands the ego's final challenge, which is the central core belief that it is the source and locus of not only identity but also of life itself. At that point, one is all alone and shorn of all protection or comforting props, belief systems, or even memory. There is solely available within one's aura the high-frequency vibration of the consciousness of the Enlightened Teacher, with its encoded Knowingness. The last step is intuited as a finality from which no turning back is possible, and thus there is consternation at the absoluteness of the finality.

Then arises the knowing to walk straight ahead, no matter what, for all fear is illusion. As this last step is taken by the Spiritual Will, death is experienced, but the fierce anguish lasts for only a few moments. The death of the ego is the only actual death that one can possibly experience, in contrast to which the previous deaths of leaving the body were relatively trivial. The experience of death is terminated by awe at the revelation of the Ultimate Reality—and then even the awe disappears and the Self transcends the duality of Existence versus Nonexistence, Allness versus Nothingness, and Omnipresence versus Void.

In the end, to the true devotee, the pursuit of spiritual reality supersedes all other considerations. The commitment to become enlightened involves the decision *No matter what.*

The serious student needs to know well in advance that at the very last doorway (Final Doorway calibrates at 999), he will be confronted by his willingness to surrender life itself—or at least that which has been believed since the beginning of evolution to be the very core of life itself. This final gateway is very rarely passed, and one reason is the lack of preparation, the lack of certainty, and a final doubt of major magnitude.

＊

At the final moment, the last vestiges of doubt and existential fear may surface from the depths. At that point, faith in the teachings of the masters that direct us to "Walk straight ahead, no matter what" arises and proves to be correct, for the glory of God awaits on the other side of the last great barrier.

＊   ＊   ＊

GLOSSARY

This glossary is a composite of edited excerpts from Dr. Hawkins's work.

Consciousness: Consciousness is the unlimited, omnipresent, universal energy field, carrier wave, and reservoir of all information available in the universe—and, more important, it is the very essence and substrate of the capacity to know or experience, to perceive or witness. Even more critically, consciousness is the irreducible, primary quality of all existence—the formless, invisible field of energy of infinite dimension and potentiality, independent of time, space, or location, yet all-inclusive and all-present.

Consciousness is an impersonal quality of Divinity expressed as awareness and is nondualistic and nonlinear. It is like infinite space that is capable of awareness, and is a quality of the Divine Essence.

Context: The total field of observation predicated by a point of view. Context includes any significant facts that qualify the meaning of a statement or event. Data is meaningless unless its context is defined. To "take out of context" is to distort the significance of a statement by failing to identify contributory accessory conditions that would qualify the inference of meaning.

Duality: The world of form characterized by seeming separation of objects, reflected in conceptual dichotomies such as "this/that," "here/there," "then/now," or "yours/mine." This perception of limitation is produced by the senses because of the restriction implicit in a fixed point of view.

Ego (or self with a small *s*): The ego is the imaginary doer behind thought and action. Its presence is firmly believed to be necessary and essential for survival. The reason is that the ego's primary quality is perception, and as such, it is limited by the paradigm of supposed causality. The ego could be called the central processing and planning center; the integrative, executive, strategic, and tactical focus that orchestrates, copes, sorts, stores, and retrieves. It can be thought of as a set of entrenched habits of thought that are the result of entrainment by invisible energy fields that dominate human consciousness. They become reinforced by repetition and by the consensus of society. Further reinforcement comes from language itself.

To think in language is a form of self-programming. The use of the pronoun "I" as the subject, and therefore the implied cause of all actions, is the most serious error and automatically creates a duality of subject and object. Put another way, the ego is a set of programs in which reason operates through complex, multilayered series of algorithms wherein thought follows certain decision trees that are variously weighted by past experience, indoctrination, and social forces; it is therefore not a self-created condition. The instinctual drive is attached to the programs, thereby causing physiological processes to come into play.

Enlightenment: A state of unusual awareness that replaces ordinary consciousness. The self is replaced by the Self. The condition is beyond time or space, is silent, and presents itself as a revelation. The condition follows dissolution of the ego. Everything is realized to be autonomous rather than the result of causality.

Karma: In essence, individual karma is an information package (analogous to a computer chip) that exists within the nonphysical domain of consciousness. It contains the code of stored information that is intrinsic to, and a portion of, the spiritual body or soul. The core represents a condensation of all past experiences, together with associated nuances of thought and feeling. The spirit body retains freedom of choice, but the range of choices has already been patterned.

Karma is linear, propagates via the soul, and is inherited as the consequence of significant acts of the will. Karma really means accountability— and, as cited in previous spiritual research, every entity is answerable to the universe. To summarize, as is commonly known, karma (spiritual fate) is the consequence of decisions of the will and determines spiritual destiny after physical death (the celestial levels, hell, purgatory, or the so-called inner astral planes [bardos]). Included also is the option of reincarnation in the human physical domain, which, by consciousness-calibration research, can only be done by agreement with the individual will. So all humans have, by agreement, chosen this pathway. In addition, consciousness research confirms that all persons are born under the most optimal conditions for spiritual evolution, no matter what the appearance seems to be. You don't get born without your approval.

Linear: Following a logical progression in the manner of Newtonian physics and, therefore, solvable by traditional mathematics through the use of differential equations.

Nonduality: When the limitation of a fixed locus of perception is transcended, there is no longer an illusion of separation nor of space and time as we know them. On the level of nonduality there is observing but no observer, as subject and object are one. You-and-I becomes the One Self experiencing all as Divine. In nonduality, consciousness experiences itself as both manifest and unmanifest, yet there is no experiencer. In this reality, the only thing that has a beginning and an ending is the act of perception itself.

Positionality: The positionalities are structures that set the entire thinking mechanism in motion and activate its content. Positionalities are programs, not the real Self. The world holds an endless array of positions that are arbitrary presumptions and totally erroneous. Primordial positionalities are: (1) *Ideas have significance and importance;* (2) *There is a dividing line between opposites;* (3) *There is a value of authorship—thoughts are valuable because they are "mine";* (4) *Thinking is necessary for control, and survival depends on control.* All positionalities are voluntary.

Self (capital *S*): The Self is beyond, yet innate in, all form—timeless, without beginning or end, changeless, permanent, and immortal. Out of it arises awareness, consciousness, and an infinite condition of "at home-ness." It is the ultimate subjectivity from which everyone's sense of "I" arises. The Infinite Reality does not even know itself as "I," but as the very substrate of the capacity for such a statement. It is invisible and all-present. The Self is the Reality of reality, the Oneness and Allness of Identity. It is the ultimate "I-ness" of consciousness itself as the manifestation of the unmanifest. Thus, only can the indescribable be described.

Subjectivity: Life is lived solely on the level of experience and none other. All experience is subjective and nonlinear; therefore, even the linear, perceptual, sequential delineation of "reality" cannot be experienced except subjectively. All "truth" is a subjective conclusion. All life in its essence is nonlinear, nonmeasurable, nondefinable. It is purely subjective.

Truth: Truth is relative and only "true" in a given context. All truth is only so within a certain level of consciousness. For instance, to forgive is commendable, but at a later stage, one sees there is actually nothing to forgive. There is no "other" to be forgiven. Everyone's ego is equally unreal, including one's own. Perception is not reality. Truth arises out of subjectivity and is obvious and self-revealing. Truth is radical subjectivity. With the collapse of the illusions of duality, including the supposed "reality" of a separate "self," there remains only the state of the Infinite "I," which is the manifestation of the Unmanifest as the Self. Truth has no opposites, such as falsity or "off-ness."

Nothing is hidden from the field of consciousness. The ultimate truth is beyond is-ness, beingness, or any intransitive verb. Any attempt at Self-definition, such as "I Am That I Am"—or even just "I Am"—is redundant. The Ultimate

Reality is beyond all names. "I" signifies the radical subjectivity of the state of Realization. It is in itself the complete statement of Reality.

ABOUT THE AUTHOR AND EDITOR

Sir David R. Hawkins, M.D., Ph.D., was an internationally renowned psychiatrist, consciousness researcher, spiritual lecturer, and mystic. He was the author of more than eight volumes, including the bestseller *Power vs. Force*, and his work has been translated into more than 17 languages. In the 1970s, he co-authored *Orthomolecular Psychiatry* with Nobel laureate Linus Pauling, revolutionizing the field of psychiatry. Dr. Hawkins made appearances on *The MacNeil/Lehrer NewsHour*, *The Barbara Walters Show*, and the *Today* show. He lectured at Westminster Abbey, the Oxford Forum, the University of Argentina, Notre Dame, Stanford, and Harvard; and has served as advisor to Catholic, Protestant, and Buddhist monasteries.

Winner of the Huxley Award, knighted by the Sovereign Order of the Hospitallers of St. John of Jerusalem, nominated for the Templeton Prize, and honored in the East with the title Tae Ryoung Sun Kak Tosa ("Foremost Teacher of the Way to Enlightenment"), Dr. Hawkins's work continues to have a profound impact on humankind.

Website: **veritaspub.com**

Scott Jeffrey is the author of numerous books, including *Creativity Revealed: Discovering the Source of Inspiration.*

Website: **scottjeffrey.com**

We hope you enjoyed this Hay House book. If you'd like to receive our online catalog featuring additional information on Hay House books and products, or if you'd like to find out more about the Hay Foundation, please contact:

Hay House, Inc., P.O. Box 5100, Carlsbad, CA 92018-5100
(760) 431-7695 or (800) 654-5126
(760) 431-6948 (fax) or (800) 650-5115 (fax)
www.hayhouse.com® • www.hayfoundation.org

———

Published in Australia by: Hay House Australia Pty. Ltd.,
18/36 Ralph St., Alexandria NSW 2015
Phone: 612-9669-4299 • *Fax:* 612-9669-4144
www.hayhouse.com.au

Published in the United Kingdom by: Hay House UK, Ltd.,
The Sixth Floor, Watson House, 54 Baker Street, London W1U 7BU
Phone: +44 (0)20 3927 7290 • *Fax:* +44 (0)20 3927 7291
www.hayhouse.co.uk

Published in India by: Hay House Publishers India,
Muskaan Complex, Plot No. 3, B-2, Vasant Kunj, New Delhi 110 070
Phone: 91-11-4176-1620 • *Fax:* 91-11-4176-1630
www.hayhouse.co.in

———

<u>**Access New Knowledge.**</u>
<u>**Anytime. Anywhere.**</u>

Learn and evolve at your own pace
with the world's leading experts.

www.hayhouseU.com

Printed in the United States
by Baker & Taylor Publisher Services